# The Secret's Secret
## Unlocking the Secrets of
## True Health and Happiness

16.05.2012

Dear Molly & Mike Mulholland
Love and all the best

© Çitlembik / Nettleberry Publications, 2012
© Özer Uçuran Çiller, 2012
The Secret's Secret: Unlocking the Secrets of True Health and Happiness

246 p.; 14x21 cm

ISBN: 978-9944-424-92-9

1.Self-actualization (Psychology).
2.Health.

LC: BF724.65.S44          DC: 156.66

Translator: Hugh Hawes
Editor: Nancy Öztürk
Illustrations: Trici Venola
Layout: Çiğdem Dilbaz

First printing, April 2012

Cover photograph rights acquired from www.istockphoto.com

Printed at Ayhan Matbaası
Mahmutbey Mah. Deve Kaldırım Cad.
Gelincik Sokak No: 6 Kat: 3 Bağcılar/İstanbul
Tel: (0212) 445 32 38
Certificate Number: 22749

In Turkey:
Şehbender Sokak 18/4
Asmalımescit - Tünel
34430 Istanbul
www.citlembik.com.tr
Certificate Number: 12369

In the USA:
Nettleberry LLC
44030 123rd St.
Eden, South Dakota 57232
www.nettleberry.com

# The Secret's Secret
## Unlocking the Secrets of
## True Health and Happiness

by ÖZER UÇURAN ÇILLER

Translated by Hugh Hawes

# Contents

# Dedication

I would like to express my heartfelt gratitude to my dear wife Tansu and to my children Mert and Berk for their love, support and critical judgment in making this book into what it is.

# Foreword

From the outset of the human story, thinkers, philosophers and scientists have attempted to find an explanation for the purpose of creation, for the fundamental dynamic of creation and for the laws that rule the cosmos, and each new approach and discovery has succeeded in reinforcing the power of this purpose.

Naturally enough, this progression continues to the present time. Our desire and need to understand the mystery of creation and its Creator have only further fueled the fire of interest of every contemplating and inquiring mind. Even if we are never completely able to understand the Creator's purpose, we will come as close as it is humanly possible to do so by focusing on the basic principles of the universe and on the "Law of Attraction" in particular.

This book is thus both an attempt to understand and explain the unique insights into the workings of the body and mind and an attempt to discover what the Law of Attraction truly reveals. It is also a scientific approach to an explanation of the "Secret" underlying our very existence. Another of the objectives of this book is to help us become aware of the "I" within us. This will impart to us the strength to achieve sound bodies and minds as we realize our every aspiration.

All of us already possess the power that can be positively

harnessed to alter our physical, emotional, mental and spiritual well-being. My purpose here is to raise our consciousness so that we become aware of this actuality; of course, this can only come about if we approach the subject with a completely open mind.

As long as we remain oblivious to the fact that the power to heal lies within us and that to realize this requires the will to reveal it, then there is no one who can be of any help to us. Being aware of the importance of evaluating, deliberating and loving ourselves is as essential to our complete health as are the emotional, mental, spiritual and physical aspects of the same.

Upon setting my course towards the heart of the "Secret" and engaging in the process of crossing an ocean of documentary inquiry, I managed to succeed in finally reaching the shores of the *Secret's Secret*. My hope here is to share this journey with you, one that will start with the ancient esoteric teachings. We will then sail through the latest discoveries of quantum physics while touching on the shores of holistic well-being before using the most advanced techniques to make us aware of the potent energy that lies within all of us; by doing thus, we will finally reach our desired destination and enjoy the fruits of our newly found discoveries.

The havens that we will visit on the way will give us an opportunity to share many different points of view and techniques so that we will truly begin to comprehend the significance of holistic health as we, at the same time, begin to learn what we must do to make our dreams come true.

This voyage is still only at the dawn of a new age. I strongly believe that as time passes we will continue to make new discoveries and together we will sail upon new seas and set foot on ever new pristine shores.

I hope that this book will be, for you as much as it has been for me, the chart to lead you to that New Age.

# I

## Life's Enigma

## The secret of existence as concealed in the law of attraction

The Law of Attraction –one which has no relation whatsoever to Newton's Law of Universal Gravitation– has become widely discussed in recent years. Just use any internet search engine and you will immediately be confronted with a vast array of information on the subject, something that would have been impossible to imagine even just a dozen or so years earlier. Add to this the wide number of books and articles that have been published on the subject during recent years and we end up almost limitless resources to support the thesis and, within minutes, find an equally rich source of opposing opinions to support its antithesis.

Thus, spending an equal amount of time researching the antithesis as well as our thesis gives us the possibility of arriving at a synthesis-based, analytical conclusion.

Despite all the resources, however, I was astonished and excited to discover that until now, no academic studies had been done on the subject. What was more, an accepted definition of the law was nowhere to be found.

Author Rhonda Byrne looked into the Law of Attraction in her best-selling book, *The Secret*. But, strikingly, while each the nineteen researchers she included in her book endeavored to find a definition for the dynamic universal secrets of the Law of Attraction, none could go any further than adding their own weight to the view that there was more than a little substance to the law itself.

The term, "Law of Attraction," though used frequently by esoteric thinkers in a variety of sources, appears not to share a common definition. Despite this, all New Age thinkers do agree that the Law of Attraction is based on the fact that "like attracts like" and consequently also agree that aspirations can be achieved by concentrating thought on the object of that desired.

This means that the individual can use his or her conscious and sub-conscious thoughts, along with their feelings and beliefs, to irrevocable change the physical world around them; but this can also mean that the outcome can be as easily negative as it is positive, and that this can transpire without the individual even being aware of it.

On the other hand, the apparently materialistic nature of this Law of Attraction and the statements made about it by its practitioners have left it open to criticism. The proponents of the Law of Attraction and the use of its definition by New Age thinkers and esotericists as a "law" are also often criticized as not being based on sufficient scientific evidence.

Despite the criticism, when looking at the historical development of the Law of Attraction it becomes clear that the ideas and beliefs behind it are far from new. Elements of the Law of Attraction, after all, can be found in Hinduism and also in Theosophy, a school of thought that has been widely influenced by Hinduism.

The Law of Attraction was first used in the modern sense as we know it by Helena Blavatsky in 1877 in her first esoteric work titled: *Isis Unveiled: Secrets of the Ancient Wisdom Tradition*. In 1879 the phrase first appeared in the media when it was used in an article in the *New York Times* on April 6 discussing the Colorado Gold Rush and the attraction of the prospectors to their fortune.

In 1902 James Allen (1864-1912) referred to the principal of the Law of Attraction, without using that term, in his work titled *As a Man Thinketh*.

In the preface to this book, Allen quotes from the *Old Testament Book of Proverbs*: 23:7 "For as he thinketh in his heart, so is he," which, put another way, means "you manifest what you believe."

In 1906, William Walker Atkinson (1862-1932) used the term in his New Thought Movement book *Thought Vibration* or the *Law of Attraction in the Thought World*. At that time, Atkinson was the editor of *New Thought Magazine* as well as being a student of Hinduism and the author of more than a hundred books on religion, spiritualism and the occult.

More recently, the release of the film, *The Secret* (2006), and the subsequent book, have generated a heightened interest in the subject and this interest increased even more when the film, book and author were featured on top-rated television shows like the *Oprah Winfrey Show*.

In September 2006 Hay House published Esther Hicks' *The Law of Attraction*, which went straight onto the New York Times Bestsellers list. 2006 also saw the publication of yet another successful book on the Law of Attraction: *The Grateful Life: Living the Law of Attraction*, by Beth and Lee McCain.

So, why did some of the greatest thinkers of all time, like Thomas Edison, Albert Einstein, Henry Ford and Andrew Carnegie, while reaping the benefits of using the Secret, never question what the Law of Attraction was? Perhaps the inventor of the telephone, Alexander Graham Bell, best summed it up: "I can't say what the Secret could be. The only thing I can say is that it exists."

\* \* \*

In the meantime, the destinies of many of the people who have come to believe in the Law of Attraction have become attached to the cosmos and its laws, and thereby the means to change the course of their lives. It is thus that many today contend that the laws of nature cannot be explained by scientific evidence alone and why the Law of Attraction must be considered in the light of the laws of Karma and even the Ten Commandments; in other words, non-scientific evidence must be taken into consideration as well.

This point of view is particularly prevalent among those who are proponents of New Thought and New Age. The shared understanding among adherents of New Thought is that the Law of Attraction is based on the use of positive affirmation and its expressions. Adherents to this new approach to the Law of Attraction also argue that quantum physics lies at the very heart of this law. Put simply, they propose that as the cognitive process produces energy, this energy attracts the energy that it resembles.

However, in this work I can only set out in the direction led me by my research and experience as I attempt to attain the knowledge of the secret of life that is the secret of the Law of Attraction itself. I will do this by investigating the question of "What is the secret's secret?"

As I set out on this arduous path I acknowledge first that there is no living person who does not want their journey through this life to pass in health, success and happiness; that being so, we can do no better than to be fully armed with an extensive knowledge of the 'secret of life".

The synthesis of our research is based on three major assumptions:

    The secret of life is the "Law of Attraction."
    The secret's secret is "resonance."
    The secret's secret secret is "to love oneself."

We will deal with each of these subjects in more detail, but we should be aware that the "Law of Attraction" has also been defined as the "Law of Similars." This is the concept of "like attracting like," or, as we will see in more detail, the belief that the results of all of our actions will sooner or later come back to us and that, one way or another, the performer of any given action will receive his or her recompense in line with the given action. This law is as true for health as it is for success and happiness. It is one of the most miraculous fundamentals of the universe and can be of vital assistance to us.

* * *

Thoughts are energy forms with magnetic properties; they also form the basis of the Law of Attraction. When we think of something we construct a field of attraction. Every thought represents a measure of energy with its own frequency of resonance. These resonances are identical to radio waves in the way that they are transmitted into the ether, where they can be drawn to a receiver tuned into the same frequency.

In turn, every transmitted thought returns to its source: to us. Positive thinking attracts positivity, negative thinking attracts negativity. Thus, an individual who lacks self-love or who is not at peace with him or herself can only produce positive thoughts of a momentary duration. In order to sustain this state and to acquire an ability to continually transmit positive energy, the individual must first attain self-love. When this is achieved, and as long as this autogenous love is maintained, that individual's life becomes a veritable series of miracles! Only in this situation can we transmit positive energy to other people and those around us, while managing the Law of Attraction so that positive events and feelings always return to us.

Loving ourselves cannot be equated with egoism and selfishness. On the contrary, some of the most noticeable effects of loving oneself include the gaining of the appreciation of others. Its other benefits include being at peace with oneself and others and being able to forgive and love others.

I will now let you in on a secret! The secret of this book—

the secret of the Law of Attraction—is "resonance" and the secret of resonance is "loving oneself." But to begin to understand the miraculous phenomenon of resonance and of loving ourselves, first let us consider the source of the secret, esotericism, by looking at excerpts from my book, *Pencere*/The Window.

## Mastering the Rudiments of the Law of Attraction and Esotericism

Many authorities say that esotericism can be best defined as "concealed teaching;" in other words, the transmission from one to another of a secret.

In esotericism the inner meanings and secrets are concealed from the uninitiated. A master of this knowledge only shares this information to a select few through means of an initiation.

This does not mean that esotericism is a religion or a belief system. It is rather a practice that holds that esoteric knowledge or inner truths and secrets are so powerful that they are not to be used by just everybody; the initiate needs a period of instruction before gaining the right to access this knowledge. Only those found fit for instruction are introduced to esoteric knowledge and are done so in a series of levels of enlightenment.

While not every individual has the capability to appreciate and understand this knowledge, no one is ever given knowledge that is beyond their ability to grasp or assimilate. This is because knowledge that cannot be assimilated can cause harm and even injure the person who is privy to it.

The importance of esotericism is that it reveals proof of the energy of thought and the power that is thereby released. Esotericism is the most striking example of the miraculous powers of the energy of thought and its knowledge base has been crucially important for all of us for it has served as the basis for most religions.

Esotericism is the light that helps to reveal the miracles that have always played an important role for both humanity and in the development of faith. How miracles can be achieved is something that has been only taught to the initiated few and is a secret kept securely behind closed doors.

Prior to their initiation, those in search of answers have always been keenly interested in how Buddhist monks levitate or how the heart of a frog can be stopped without physical contact; and in telekinesis, how objects can achieve unassisted movement. Now recent revelations about this knowledge have given further credence to the proof of the power of the mind as this knowledge continues to open new doors for man. Today's scientific research dedicated to proving the power of the mind is also bringing us a new understanding of the powers inherent in our minds and in the relationship of this power to vibrational medicine.

Quite recently a piece of electronic equipment was shown to the media at the Paris "European Research and Discovery Fair." Its American inventors claim that it can read brain waves; in other words the device is capable of reading our thoughts.

The generic name of this Brain-Computer-Interface is BCI. The latest generation of this technology demonstrates how a paralyzed patient can, while wired up to the device, manipulate a computer keyboard by simply visualizing the letters. This person can thus write and send coherent email messages. The significance of this discovery is that, for example, fully paralyzed individuals will be able to communicate their daily requirements unhindered.

There has been wide media coverage of how some paralyzed patients, after being taught biofeedback techniques, have also been able to overcome their disabilities just by using the power of thought. It has become apparent that in this century physicians will be more motivated to draw on the esoteric principals that make up a large part of vibrational medicine.

\* \* \*

But while we are going to attempt to open a few of those doors here, we must remember that throughout history the dissemination of this knowledge has been strictly controlled; it was feared that the irresponsible use of these secrets could lead to the degeneration of humanity. We will thus proceed slowly and carefully into our discoveries.

Let us first look back in time. Let us for a while ignore the recent scientific discoveries and look back to the origin of esotericism: According to one rather imaginative view, it may have originated from the Mu civilization (people of a universe of infinite stars). Proponents of this view hold that these people were in fact partially galactic in origin and, in displaying their miraculous abilities to both initiated and non-initiated, they may have demolished the values of the society in which they lived. Others who have deeply contemplated the power of the mind have considered esotericism as a process of becoming closer to the Divine Being. According to yet other accounts, three of the prophets and three of the world's major religions had their origins in esotericism.

While, however, proposing different ideas about its origin, all do agree that the miraculous power of the mind occurs through focus and intense concentration and that mystics with para-psychic abilities like telepathy, telekinesis, levitation, clairvoyance, and astral projection can successfully harness all these powers.

## Questioning Quantum

One of the world's foremost professors of quantum physics, Fred Alan Wolf, was interviewed by the media on the nature of quantum physics; he also happens to be one of the contributors to Byrne's book *The Secret*. This professor has also achieved some prominence with a film that focuses on a similar concept, "What the *bleep* Do We Know?" He also has other documentaries to his credit.

Following is a translated extract from an interview with

Prof Wolf for the Turkish *Milliyet* daily newspaper, in which he explains the basic principals of quantum:

> …Whenever we observe anything and as soon as that observation commences, this very action will, wanted or not, affect the thing being observed.
>
> In other words, we can affect change merely by observation.
>
> Generally in this situation we could state that we create our own reality. This ability extends to a point where we can control what the future will hold, but of course, this can never be one hundred per cent assured.
>
> There isn't a single person on this planet who can control either their own or another's destiny. This is because we are all interconnected: to each other, to the earth, to the planets, to the sun, to the stars, to the universe, to everything. There are always different probabilities and none of us can always attain the probability that we desire.
>
> Do not look to quantum physics for the answer to the question of whether there is or is not a God. However, when we observe the physical world I believe that we can maintain that a "Quantum Intelligence" or a "Conscious Domain" exists and that this Conscious Domain exists in reality.
>
> Apart from the individual intelligence that each individual carries in his or her own body, there can be said to be a universal intelligence that we could, for sake of argument, call "Divine Intelligence." However, it must be pointed out that quantum physics does not concern itself with either theology or with mysticism…

Prof. Wolf went on to give a striking example of how "we affect reality by observing it":

> …When you look into the mirror you might, for example, think that you are ugly. But if someone were to appear who was to find you very attractive, the reality of finding yourself

ugly would begin to change. In fact, you would begin to feel attractive. This is how your life can be changed and what direction it will take and the effect it will have on you.

The determiner, as Prof. Wolf quite rightly says, is just how we perceive ourselves in the mirror. Is it one day attractive and one day ugly? Or is it always ugly or indefinitely beautiful? Do we like ourselves one day and dislike ourselves the next? It is important to be aware that the way we see ourselves reflects the way we are. If we honestly appraise our interior world and appreciate ourselves for who we are, we will consequently love ourselves and this will become our reality. But we must be completely aware of the truth of our own reality.

This is because from that moment forward, that is exactly what the mirror will always reflect. And this becomes our potential to be the "conscious domain" or part of the "quantum intelligence." We should remember, however, that everything we accept as real and unchanging can, in fact, be changed.

If we wish to be surrounded by affection we must first love ourselves. If this is the reality we consistently wish to experience, we must maintain our defense of our "quantum intelligence" against both internal and external threats. If only it were as easy to live life like this as it is to describe it! But if life were that easy, would we see ourselves surrounded by so many unhappy people?

Everything in the universe is energy.
Our thoughts are particles of energy.
There are endless probabilities in our lives.
In the quantum field in which we find ourselves everything affects everything else.

All the radiated energy from the particles of our thought generates a response.

The essential point is that the frequency of the energy radiated from our thoughts must find a response from quantum particles of a similar frequency.

To realize this and to receive what we desire we must create a quantum field.

\* \* \*

It would be difficult for anyone to have avoided hearing about Byrne's book *The Secret*. Not only did it climb to the top of charts world –wide, in the first weeks of being published in Turkey it sold over two hundred thousand copies, a rare event indeed in Turkey's publishing world. This book can be summarized thusly: "Life's great secret is the Law of Attraction," with the Law of Attraction being defined as "like attracts like." Whatever our thoughts are concerning any given subject–we–by association–attract similar thoughts back to ourselves. This is the essence of the book. As far as the details are concerned, they have already been covered by those with a greater knowledge of quantum physics. It is a book from which everyone can benefit and for some it has become the first book to which they turn.

Despite its wide appeal, it is a book that has also attracted heavy criticism. Interestingly enough, heading the list of critics is Professor Wolf himself. Again, during his visit to Turkey, he had this to say about *The Secret*:

...a very well-packaged piece of folly. People are led to believe there is a secret and when they learn this secret they will be able to possess the wealth or person of their desires. This can bring happiness to no one. Think about it; if everyone won the lottery, the payout would become insignificantly small. The lucky ones would always win.

Prof. Wolf went on to say that when interviewed for his contributions to the book a great deal of what he had said on this subject had been edited out and that the book did not reveal any secrets of how to turn desires into reality. He added: "I told them that I didn't even understand my own reality."

He concluded the *Milliyet* interview by saying that *The Secret* has no relation to quantum physics whatsoever and apart from one contributor teacher, none of the other contributors had any knowledge of quantum physics.

If one were to paraphrase what Prof. Wolf had said, it would be something like this: *If one were to observe reality it would appear to change. Quantum physics reveals that you can create your own reality; its form can change and everything can take on a different aspect.*

*You can compare this to our different opinions of a painting in an exhibition. You can expand on the painting's flaws, or you can focus on what you admire and what delights you. However much our approval is based on visual appraisal, our approach and our purpose in many areas becomes the criteria for the way in which we express ourselves.*

*It is no accident that we often find ourselves interacting with people who are like us, who share the same interests and have the same outlook on life. When the Secret is viewed from this angle it appears less complex; it is simply a manifestation of "like attracts like."*

## Homeopathy and Resonance Therapy

The concept of "like attracts like" is also the basis of vibrational medicine and the highest profile application of what we know about homeopathy, a form of medicine that was formulated in Germany before gaining popularity around the world. Ranking as one of the oldest branches of complementary medicine, homeopathy is derived from two ancient Greek words, "like" and "suffering"; its basic premise is to treat an illness with a medication known to produce similar symptoms.

Homeopathic remedies are part of vibrational medicine in that they carry the vibrational imprint or data of a plant or mineral in infinitesimal proportions.

A newer form of vibrational medicine is a kind of therapy termed *Biological Resonance Therapy*. This therapy model uses special equipment to locate and focus on the malfunctioning frequency of the patient's condition. That frequency is then corrected and the patient's condition returned to normal. In this case its relationship to "like attracts like" is that "like heals like" and the law of attraction thus becomes a powerful weapon in the armory of medicine.

I will deal with the practices of homeopathy and biological resonance in more detail in the Vibrational Medicine chapter of this book but, suffice to say, both treatments are both functional and practical applications of the Secret.

* * *

I am always proud to say that I am a descendant of the preeminent mystic and poet Rumi [Mavlana Jalaluddin Rumi (R.A.) 1207-1273] whose writings revealed his awareness of the Secret and exposed its miraculous reality:

> You are what you think.
> The rest is just flesh and bones.
> Think of a rose and become a rose garden.
> Think of a thorn and become a brier patch.

Could there be a better definition of the Secret's Secret? Let us proceed, with the hope that our thoughts will always be of roses!

# II

## The Existence of Life

Before beginning an analytical account of the Secret, it might be worthwhile to make a brief overview of some of the written references made to and about the existence of life.

To fully conceptualize the existence of life we must ask a number of vital questions, and we must not overlook the importance of their theoretical and conceptual aspects when we attempt an explanation.

- How can the Big Bang theory be explained?
- Following the Big Bang, how did living cells manage to evolve from mineral molecules?
- How did life begin?
- How did the human race emerge on earth? What substance is there in the Hologenesis view? That is, that humans emerged in a number of different locations and not just in one, and is it a credible argument?
- What is the secret behind the existence of the universe and humanity?
- What is the nature of the conflict between science and religion that surfaces from time to time?

If we could only reveal the life particle that emerged after the Big Bang, would this have to be an answer based only on reason or would we find ourselves on the path of theology?

However much Nobel laureate Leon Lederman might insist on calling the "Higgs Particle" (named after the Scottish scientist Prof. Peter Higgs) the "God particle," does it really mean that the divine hand will be revealed when it is finally isolated?

CERN (European Nuclear Research Center) was built 54 years ago on the Franco-Swiss border close to Geneva, with the objective of disclosing the secrets of the universe's creation and construction. With the former in mind, the immense Large Hadron Collider (LHC) was constructed to recreate on a microscopic level the conditions of the Big Bang and analyze the secrets revealed. By colliding and shattering charged protons in the LHC it is hoped that the hypothetical primordial particles of the universe's moment of existence, the Higgs particle, will be revealed.

The entire experiment has been designed to reveal the so-called God Particle. Up until this moment the smallest particles observed have been the sixteen particles that make up the atom: the electrons, the neutron and proton. But the outstanding question—how matter acquires its mass—remains unanswered.

It is hoped that the LHC experiment will reveal an observation of the Higgs particle, thus empirically proving the "Higgs" hypothesis that these are indeed the elemental particles, which is why they were given the sobriquet of the God particles. The results of this experiment are imminent but no one knows for sure if the God particle will be revealed.

The divine system that created the universe reflects an intelligent design. According to the standard model, the radiation dispersed by the Big Bang was absorbed by these divine—or God—information particles, thus forming matter and anti-matter. The God and anti-matter particles then disappeared in the first one-trillionth second following this Big Bang. Following this disappearance, energy obtained mass.

In my opinion, matter was created by the fusion of God and anti-matter particles with energy. In short, these particles were not destroyed, but rather they themselves became part of matter by giving form to matter. In other words, both matter and anti-matter became masked within what we know as "matter." In fact, it is being asserted that when matter was made to collide together in CERN, scientists were able to observe anti-matter for 15 minutes and were able to thus track the traces of the God particles, or Higgs particles.

The atoms that gained or lost electrons due to the disappearance of anti-matter particles gained movement in this newly-ionized form. It was this movement that caused the God information particles to become the basic determinants in the universe and in life. Despite this, CERN does not yet speak of the possibility that the God particles carry divine, or God-inspired, information. As Professor John Archibald Wheeler has expressed it, the theory of physics rests on the concept of "information." It is thus that the cosmic laws carried by the divine system gave rise to the evolutionary process that is the information-based universe. This leads us to understand the following:

"Everything in the universe is energy directed by Divine information."

Does this mean that all these resources and effort are just being used to find the God particle? Will the creationists declare victory if the God particle be found in this experiment? Or would those on the other side say that this simply eminently demonstrates the complex beauty of the universe? Or, what of those in the middle, the physicists and theologians, who speak of two different Divine Beings; one, of the divine fingerprint in the laws of physics and the other, of the divine presence in supplication?

There are three views that define these standpoints. The

first is "intelligent design;" the second is the "theory of evolution;" and the third is a series of "rational events."

## Intelligent Design and the Theory of Evolution

There are two camps when it comes to explaining the development of life within the universe; some religions and followers of esotericism speak of "intelligent design," while the rationalists defend natural selection and Darwinian theory.

Those who lay claim to this series of rational events have a tendency to state that it is close to an acceptable reality because of their observations of the same; however, those who support Darwin's theories have no explanation as to how and why the first single cell life started. Up until this moment no one has been able to recreate as much as one cell in laboratory conditions. It appears that such a complex and perfect life system of even a proto-cell could not have evolved merely through chance.

It is hypothesized that the universe is 15 billion years old and the prevalent theory maintains that it started with the Big Bang. Life is thought to have begun on earth comparatively soon after the planet cooled down.

Those who support the concept of Intelligent Design propose that the universe and life were created by a "Divine Creator." In other words, human existence came about as a result of design; those who support this proposal cannot accept that it could have been as a chance occurrence in the process of the universe. But when it comes to the starting point of matter, the God particle, neither the creationists nor the scientific rationalists can come up with a scientific explanation. In fact, some creationists will go as far as to state that this concept has no religious base at all. However, those faiths that have embraced esoteric teaching are comfortable with this concept within their ideas of creation.

Harold Maurer wrote a thought-provoking book on the existence of life called *The Principle of Existence*. Maurer proposes that the world was designed in accordance with Einstein's theory of relativity, but that the phenomenon of existence had not been sufficiently explained. He goes on to criticize those who contend that convincing explanations for Einstein's absolute speed of light, gravity and DNA have been largely overlooked. Maurer explains that behind every enigma and every secret there are two explanations: one is complex and one is simple.

Maurer attempts to explain the principle of existence from a philo-physicist point of view, by combining the science of existence with philosophical elements and finding the reasoning between intelligent and physical events. He suggests that even those who accept the existence of God, despite the ingenious complexity of the cosmos, speak as though "It" functioned as a simple but glorious automatic machine.

The most striking argument of Maurer's book is when he equates the shapeless, formless and featureless nature of existence with something he has named TAO (The Absolute Organization). He proposes that it is possible to speculate and hypothesize about TAO with relation to the existence of the universe, but it cannot be defined.

Maurer goes on to say that however desperately and unsuccessfully science tries to find the reason behind existence, and however difficult it is to give TAO a scientific definition, one thing remains clear: TAO was there from the very beginning. Maurer then lists how the other principles of existence reinforce this.

These principles suggest that when one accepts TAO acting as a base for energy and data, then a whole number of scientific explanations emerge. Maurer proposes that the universe did not necessarily start with Einstein's theory of relativity or the Big Bang theory but he, rather, directs our attention to other possibilities. Although he rather modestly describes himself as an "investigative writer" he also displays the authority of a Nobel laureate in physics when he offers an inspired scientific explanation of all the principles of existence that remain outside TAO.

While Maurer emphasizes that "behind every conundrum there can always be found a simple explanation" it can still be difficult to grasp the principals to which he refers without a strong grounding in quantum physics. However, there are great rewards for anyone who makes the effort.

To summarize, Maurer devised the name TAO to describe the source of existence that is made up solely of energy; he refers only to its vibrational properties, not to any suggestion that it oscillates, but that it resides in all the details of the principles of existence.

## Divine and Non-Divine Religions

If we approach the existence of life from a theological point of view we observe that, generally speaking, there are two separate beliefs. The first group is made up of religions and philosophies that do not require a godhead creator, while for the second group the godhead is paramount.

In beliefs such as Taoism, Confucianism and Buddhism, there are no references to a creator; neither is a creator revered. Instead of references to the existence of life, emphasis is placed on the individual's morality and actions. For example, Taoism references the three jewels of compassion, moderation, and humility, around which this quasi-religion is constructed, while Buddhism focuses on the essence of awareness, conscience and knowledge as the foundation of its belief system.

Among the divine religions, despite there being many subdivisions, there are generally four different belief categories that are referred to: Theism, Deism, Atheism and Pantheism.

- *Theism* can be summarized as the conception of a Divine Being who is personal and active in the creation, governance and organization of the universe and world, directing humanity through the revelation of prophets.

- *Deism* describes a belief in a Divine Being as a creator who does not require the help of prophets and, apart from creating the universe, life and humanity, takes no further part in its existence.
- *Atheists* reject any form of Divine Being and attempt to prove this by rational scientific means. Richard Dawkins, the author of many books including The Selfish Gene and The God Delusion, is an example of a well-known scientist who professes atheism.
- *Pantheism* was first defined in the modern age by the 17th century philosopher Baruch Spinoza. Spinoza proposed that everything is one and the one is the Divine Being and that the name of the Divine Being and nature are the same and define reality. There is more than a little esotericism in his work as he describes a belief system whereby the universe and the Divine Being are one interdependent entity. Esotericism, as we have already noted, is a system of knowledge that is confined to the initiated. Pantheism is by its very nature monotheist and regards the esoteric secrets such as telepathy, telekinesis, clairvoyance, levitation and astral projection as essential elements of that belief and are elements it frequently calls upon..

Theosophy is a more recent tradition, with roots in pantheism and philosophy; it draws heavily on Eastern mysticism and the relationship between humanity, the cosmos and the Divine Being. Although considered a Western doctrine, theosophy could rightly be considered Eastern in tradition, as it draws heavily on esoteric knowledge.

For the theosophists, existence and the Creator are not approached through prophets but through their own powers. This explains why so many thinkers, philosophers and scientists, though traveling on different paths and at different times, are considered part of the theosophical tradition. Just a few of many examples, Rumi, Al-Farabi, Spinoza, Cicero, Thomas Edison and Halil Gibran, give a clear indication of the gravitas of this theory's proponents.

I have attempted to give a brief but enlightening insight into the philosophical concepts of theosophy with their reference to the existence of life. However theologians and theosophists have yet to construct a scientific platform on which they can meet to discuss the creation of the universe or the Divine Being. Let us hope that we will not have to wait too long before this meeting can take place and all the different disciplines can embrace in the joy and excitement of the divine.

## Information and the Cosmos

The three cornerstones of the universe are energy, matter and information.

Form comes into being within energy fields.

Form's modified function is that of in-form-ation.

The etymology of information is 'to give shape to."

It is information that gives shape to matter.

If information can give shape to matter and by association, energy, this means it can also do the same to people. If we accept this hypothesis, what does that do for Darwin's theory of evolution?

The theory of evolution states that life on earth came about and developed as a result of random events. Over time organisms evolved and changed; those living now are different from their predecessors. Evolution suggests that all life is in perpetual flux and fossil remains support that claim. We often observe that there is a tendency for supporters of Darwin's theories to be of an atheist persuasion, believing the universe too, to have been created completely randomly.

However, scientists who support the idea of "intelligent design" do so with the belief that there was an "intelligence" involved in the design and creation of the universe and life. They support their argument by alleging that Darwin's theories completely fail to explain how life, at its single cell level, actually started on earth.

Creationists cannot accept that the extraordinary and miraculously intricate system of life's cells could have come about by a random chemical reaction. Like Darwin's supporters, Creationists hold that a form of evolutionary development of organisms probably took place over time.

There is no consensus on how the first proto-cells emerged as life and came into being. Creationists defend their beliefs by saying that this transformation was a product of "intelligent design," while rationalists claim that these living cells emerged as a result of random conditions. On the other hand, my belief is that life started by Divine information, a subject on which I dwelled in detail in my book Infotheism: Divine Information.

The important contribution to what we are exploring here is that both sides agree that life on earth evolved over a period of time. Though Creationists cannot be shaken in their belief that the universe was designed and brought into existence by the Creator; and while rationalists insist that the universe was not a managed event but one of complete chance, it is useful to note that these two schools of thought actually do agree on the emergence into existence of the universe and life: both camps agree that life began with a 'thought," by which we mean information.

Whether it was "directed" or "random," the existence of the universe and more importantly, life, began in a morphogenic field. The real question here is this: where exactly did this "thought" come from?

As a result of the Big Bang, how did TAO (The Absolute Organization), perceived as an endless energy mass vibrating but with no oscillating properties, transmit this information to begin the existence of the universe and life?

It is on this point that rationalists feel completely helpless. Creationists are more comfortable with this and allege that it is self-evident: the information came from the Creator. There are also many who try to bridge the gap by pointing out that these laws of physics are merely the Creator's laws, which is why they amaze us with their miraculous order—of which humanity and the universe are but a part. Perhaps it is difficult to characterize a creator in scientific terms but like the creationists, when we are confronted with the miraculous nature of the universe, it is not so very difficult to sense a Creator's presence.

I spoke of the three cornerstones of the universe, energy, matter and information, but if there had been only the first two it would have been impossible for the universe and cellular life to begin and take form without the program that information provides.

This is why, as we resolve the secrets of the Law of Attraction and resonance, we find it easier to conceptualize the significance of "thought" or, put another way, "information."

In short, every development within the universe starts with a "thought," that is to say, information.

Thought occupies a morphic field. Morphic fields are sub-atomic and directly affect the potentiality of other fields. The result is that information creates a totality with energy and matter.

The neutron, which is 10,000 times smaller than the entire atom, lies at the center of the atom. When atoms collide at high speed the neutrons can also collide, either ricocheting off each other or impacting together to form a new neutron. At the same time sub-atomic (or rather, sub-neutron) particles can also break off. These powerful particles can reach speeds close to the speed of light at 300,000 kps. These particles form the morphic field and fulfill their role as a medium for the transfer of information.

Potential fields are characterized thus:

Potential fields retain no intrinsic power.

While they have the potential to do so, until they are brought into existence, potential fields are inactive, concealed, unrealized and undeveloped. In short, potential signifies capacity and a yet to be realized intensity.

For example, the potential energy that exists outside the cell (for instance, in nerve or muscle cells) is an electric potential created outside the cell by the cell itself. In concentrated areas of nerve or muscle tissue many cells have a stored electric potential that produces the impulses for the area's communication system. These, the body's impulses, can be detected, measured and recorded with special equipment.

The biologist Prof. Rupert Sheldrake has researched and written extensively on this subject, describing it as a memory; that is, the information retained by the brain that exists from conception.

Most of the laws that are termed "laws of nature" can be perceived as nature's reflexes, the Law of Attraction is among these. The Law of Attraction is a universal law and is the same for everyone, everywhere and always. Of the essence here is how we can harness the Law of Attraction and bring it into our own lives.

> It is essential to note here the principle of, "Whatever we resonate with, we will attract."

In order to be able to resonate correctly we need to have a sufficient accumulation of affirmative energy in our bodies.

# III

# The Secret's Scientific Explanation and the Secret's Secret

In most of the books about the "Secret," or the "Law of Attraction," the explanations "the law of similars" or "like attracts like" are given, implying that when we focus our thoughts on something we will attract the same to ourselves.

In short, the "secret" consists of recycling the stored affirmations of positive energy in our conscious and sub-conscious that have been built up through meditation and supplication into reality.

Most writers recommend a similar methodology to achieve this result. Our wishes and expectations, whether in love, health or money, are mapped out in our consciousness. In a calm and considered way we meditated on them and continue to repeat that action. By doing this our motives and action plans are directed and strengthened. All that remains is for the Law of Attraction to do its work.

Our thoughts, both negative and positive, one way or another will eventually return to us. It should be stressed that all our requests and supplications must be felt as a deep internal desire. The purpose of all thoughts and feelings is to turn our subconscious into an energy storage facility, while at the same time keeping its frequency at the highest possible level. Our high frequency affirmative thoughts will also return to us as other high frequency affirmative thoughts. The potential to achieve our desires or wishes will increase accordingly. At the same time our thoughts will cover a wider area in the quantum universe so that the chances of a match will increase as well.

From the esoteric age to the present, the Law of Attraction, or the "secret" if you prefer, appears to have left the realm of secrecy and is now firmly ensconced in the public domain. Despite the depth of research conducted in quantum physics, scientific explanations for the Law of Attraction remain inadequate.

The same thing is true of medicine; any scientific research on the efficacy of homeopathy and biological resonance is difficult to find. Most doctors who are practitioners of these treatments rely on their own experience and accumulated knowledge as, unfortunately, there is scant scientific support.

* * *

I have a private interest in—and have devoted a considerable amount of my own time to—the medical treatments facilitated by Biological Energy equipment and techniques. As a result of my research on biological resonance, I am convinced that the Law of Attraction is in fact a "resonance phenomenon." The application of the resonance phenomenon removes energy blockages in various parts of the body and allows the subtle life energy to oscillate and circulate.

The information stimuli transmitted by our whole body—and by that we include the etheric, emotional, intelligent and spiritual bodies as well as the physical—are through resonance, all elements of body's defenses that transmit through the matrix to the body's organs. This is why our bodies respond to synergic treatment, and this is the basis of biological resonance therapy. In later sections we will refer to mechanical, morphic and divine justice resonance.

Biological resonance describes the Law of Attraction's role in human health; mechanical resonance is its destructive role; morphic resonance affects behavior among species, while divine justice resonance defines the retribution system between humanity and the universe.

At the heart of both homeopathy and biological resonance is the concept of "like attracts like" or more correctly in this instance, "like attracts like and heals," revealing once again the Law of Attraction.

Let us now take a closer look at homeopathy, a form of medicine based on biological resonance: Although homeopathy has existed since antiquity in one form or another, it was not given a scientific footing until the German physician, Samuel Hahnemann (1755-1843), began to study and practice the subject. He is now considered its pioneer. Hahnemann is known for classifying pharmaceuticals into two categories, homeopathic and not homeopathic (allopathic).

Approximately fifty years after Hahnemann's death, the most important allopathic pharmaceutical, aspirin, was discovered by Hahnemann's compatriot, a 29 year-old doctor called Felix Hoffman. Considered to be the first allopathic drug, aspirin served to enhance Hahnemann's standing in the medical world.

There are now many doctors who claim to practice homeopathy; unfortunately few are aware that its basis is biological resonance and the medical world does not yet fully understand the significance of this. This is true despite the fact that Dr Hahnemann used the general description of the law of similars as the principle of the "secret" and demonstrated quite clearly that homeopathy is a biological resonance process. An approach to homeopathy could actually be seen as a bridge between conventional or orthodox medicine and vibrational medicine.

When the active makeup of homeopathic remedies is formulated to be the same as the energy frequency of the body, a resonance occurs whereby the correct vibrational mode is achieved. However, the preparation's active ingredient is not a physical one. Homeopathic remedies retain the energy frequency or the vibrational characteristic of the plant or mineral ingredients used (but not the ingredients themselves) and are an example of vibrational medicine.

Homeopathic remedies are prepared in such a way that they mirror the symptoms of the condition to be treated (in other words, approximating the same vibrational frequency), thus creating artificial symptoms that simulate the resonance and thus stimulate the body's natural defense or immune systems. This can be compared with immunization, where an inert composition of the disease-causing vector is given to the patient, providing the immune system with information necessary to stimulate a state of preparedness. Vaccines create a chemical response in the physical cells, whereas homeopathic remedies replicate the condition's frequency or vibrational modes.

Homeopathy has been accused by some of being a practice of subterfuge and fabrication. The most common accusation is that homeopathy is merely a placebo effect. The placebo effect is actually a resonance occurrence, convincing the patient that the remedy will make them better. By thinking so the energy released removes an energy blockage. The placebo effect is something to be embraced but unfortunately many orthodox physicians do not take this view and they belittle it.

Unlike homeopathic remedies that utilize energy frequency structures to treat the body, electro-biological resonance therapies work to (re)normalize the internal frequencies of the individual patient. With this form of treatment, the patient's electronic stimuli are amplified and retransmitted back to the patient, thus increasing the capacity for the body to heal itself.

This practice of biological resonance is referred to as "System Information Therapy" or SIT. This is the basis of the electro-biofeedback used to correct the individual's internal frequencies. In biological resonance therapy, biological resonance instruments are used to detect and focus on the infirm parts of the body. When the problem is located by finding the same frequency it is then treated by impulses so that the body responds, strengthening the immune system, and the patient gains the capability to heal him or herself.

In a seminar he gave in Turkey called "Diagnostic and Therapeutic Fundamentals in Modern Holistic Medicine" Dr. Darko Mardjetko said:

"When a medical condition arises in our bodies we cannot expect a full recovery without regulation (correction of vibration and oscillation) of all deficiencies.
"For example, if we do not treat the broken energy field of a patient with a malignant tumor or cancer using biological resonance or matrix regeneration therapy, the immune system will remain weak and the possibility of new cancerous growth in the same area or another weak point will remain extremely high."

This type of vibrational medicine, whereby bio-feedback biological resonance equipment is used, is particularly successful in the treatment of addictions to alcohol and tobacco.
There are two basic applications of resonance therapy in vibrational medicine. The first is to remove health problems by regulating and correcting the body's imbalance. This is called "regulation" or "correction." The second application is to remove or neutralize the detrimental factors of regulation from our bodies. This is called "inversion."
In "inversion" therapy the oscillation or frequency of the patient's cells is redirected by 180 degrees and returned back to the patient. By doing this, pathological frequencies are neutralized, thus aiding the patient's recovery.
The German natural medicine expert Oliver Schöpf provides this explanation of "regulation" and "inversion":

"Regulation is the correcting of disorders of the body, while "inversion" is the elimination of bodily disorders."

Complementary medical literature describes in detail the problems associated with energy oscillations and the resulting bio-electric blockages. If a metaphor for regulation is necessary, let us imagine this scenario: Think of a lazy child who refuses to clean his or her room even when repeatedly instructed to do so, until the day the parent shouts at the top of their voice, "Straighten up your room or else!" With this the child realizes the seriousness of the situation and begins to keep the room clean.

Inversion can be characterized as this: Imagine it is raining heavily and you have fallen asleep because you have grown accustomed to its sound (exactly the same metaphor for chronic disease or addiction). But when the rain stops and the noise is no longer there, you wake up. The lack of sound becomes a stimulation impulse for you.

Oliver Schöpf offers examples for the two treatment methods: When a part of the physical body malfunctions, the issue acts as a trigger (in the child example) and the immune system activates. In the inversion example, the defense mechanism has failed to activate, as in the case of chronic illness or energy blockages, so it is activated by the transmitting of an impulse to remove the threat and kick-start the defense mechanism. In both cases the objective is to stimulate the immune system post-resonance and holistically correct the body. As long as we regard our bodies as a whole or holistically, we will overcome illness and remain healthy. The most important element to holistic health is our immune system. The type of treatments carried out by biological resonance equipment can, in actual fact, be done by the mind alone.

Later in this book we will go into far more detail concerning the phenomenal powers of thought. We will see the extraordinary physical things achieved by a completely paralyzed patient by just using the trained mind.

- Thought is energy.
- The power of the secret is concealed within the energy of thought.
- Exactly in the same way as biological resonance equipment, our thoughts too create an electromagnetic wave field.

We have elevated sensory capabilities due to transmission of electromagnetic waves created by the electrical responses of the neurons in our brains. By utilizing the energy of thought, we can use our bodies as biological resonance equipment. Our bodies are as powerful as any radio or television transmitter and receiver. All we need to do is to learn how to control the frequency of our thoughts and the way to achieve this is by learning which thought matrices to apply. With our minds consistently in affirmation mode we can control the frequency of the thought and effectively increase its volume.

We come upon an affirmation used in this sense by the eminent metaphysicist, Mildred Mann (1904-1971) who spoke about this in her book *Seven Steps in Demonstration;* the author first mentioned affirmation in what could be considered the book's first draft: *Become What You Believe.*

Mann discusses the seven steps to achieving this, namely:

1. Desire: You must enthusiastically, excitedly, keenly and longingly imagine everything you have ever wanted in your life and have yet to obtain.
2. Be decisive: You must be clear about exactly what you want and what you wish to possess.
3. Request: You must (if you can check your enthusiasm) make your request in clear simple language.
4. Believe: You must believe in your success with your entire conscious and sub-conscious mind—with your whole being.
5. Work: In order to realize what you wish to possess you must work at it for a few minutes each day.
6. Gratitude: Your heart must be always full of thanks and you must always say in remembrance: "thank you my Creator."
7. Joyful Expectation: You must always feel yourself in happy expectation.

We must always find a way to achieve this and then have complete faith in it. We can think of this as a gift from someone and possessing it as a form of acceptance. Whatever the problem is, leave it and turn to the Creator and from the One, goodness desire. Always stay turned towards the One and you will see the Secret lies within conscientious supplication.

Mildred Mann has ten succinct phrases that we could do well to commit to memory:

- YOU ARE in the spirit of the Creator.
- YOU ARE a child of the Creator.
- YOU ARE master of all the dominant aspects of life.
- YOU ARE never alone; the Creator is always with you.
- With the Creator everyone can achieve their potential.
- Let all your words and deeds be held in affirmative thought.
- Even if you can't love your neighbor, at be aware of the Creator's presence in them.
- Even if they don't want it, make sure you give everybody something of yourself.

Meditate every day.

As we have seen, the secret of the Law of Attraction is "like attracts like" or as interpreted in healing, "like heals like." "Like attracts like" and "like heals like" are two sides of the same coin because resonance is the uniting factor. Everything in the universe is in vibration and has a resonance, like a ringing and tinkling sound that has its footing in quantum science. If we consider our thoughts in the same way, their resonance can attract other people's thoughts. This is because all energy is held within what could be described as the internal and endless reaches of the sea of the universe.

As energy cannot be destroyed, the energy of our thoughts in some small way shapes the form of the universe. This is the foundation of the Secret that has, for thousands of years, been approached with suspicion and dismissed as lacking empirical proof. If the book *The Secret* can sell millions of copies it is in no small part due to the ongoing research in quantum physics affirming much of what is written there. This is because "like attracts like" and "like heals like" have both been demonstrated to be based in "resonance."

In resonance there is an accumulation of energy in both attraction and the amplified vibration, as well as in the amplitude of the oscillation. Similarly, by increasing the frequency, the build-up of energy in our thoughts can be used for clearing energy blockages. The factors supporting "like attracts like" are the same universal natural forces such as gravity, electrical energy and electromagnetic fields. The polarity within the human organism is another factor in the Law of Attraction.

Using the power of our thoughts to demonstrate "like attracts like," it is possible to realize our desires and requests. We will discern affirmation if we think affirmatively, affection if we think affectionately, and favor and compassion from those around us if we think compassionately and favorably.

On the other hand, we will find apathy if we think apathetically; if we think evil we will attract evil; if we break another's heart our own heart will be broken; and if we commit criminal acts, we eventually reap the consequences and learn about divine justice or karma.

Affirmative resonance fills up our bodies' energy depots and with this high-frequency energy we can overcome any problem, every imbalance, every health disorder. Homeopathy and biological resonance draw on the same principal of "like heals like" and gives us an important road map for our health.

With the help of the therapies that these methods employ, we can remove the energy blockages that hinder the oscillation of our bodies' life energy, thus providing a correct diagnosis and gradually finding scientific acceptance. This is particularly true with chronic illness where conventional medicine offers little help, like chronic pain, migraine, allergies and functional disorders.

The quantum understanding is that there is that thought and design come first and are followed by a resultant action or operation. Everyone who has a holistic view of the world must be aware of this; they must accept and apply it.

## Resonance

Because we are building our knowledge base about the "secret" in small increments, we may now summarize what we have discussed thus far: We have, from the beginning, referred to the 'secret' as the Law of Attraction. We considered the associated "law of similars" of which the principles are, "like attracts like" and "like heals like."

We then considered examples of the Law of Attraction and attempted to explain the "secret" and how when revealed it carries significance of paramount importance for our spiritual and physical well-being as well as for our health. We emphasized that this has now found a general acceptance among the populace. However, there was one detail that escaped our attention; namely, what exactly is the "secret's" Law of Attraction?

Perhaps we overlooked this question because we immediately assumed that the answer was 'something similar to the laws of gravity' and left it at that. However, the real reason for a lack of detail on the nature of the Law of Attractions is a lack of sufficient scientific research. But what could possibly lie behind the Law of Attraction?

The objective of this book is, first and foremost, to illuminate as much as is humanely possible the Secret's Secret, and in doing so inform and demonstrate how we can use its application in our everyday lives. The extensive research and evaluation that I have done in preparing this book have revealed that the Secret's Secret is nothing more than a resonance phenomenon.

Resonance is created by the different frequencies that have the magnitude of maximum magnetic oscillation in energy, thus having resonant properties. Resonance is the most important principle of "the law of similars" and has been used in homeopathic treatments for centuries. The starting point was the etymology of the word homeopathy, which in ancient Greek can indicate "like suffering"; the treatment of a disorder with something that produces similar symptoms.

If we accept that the "secret" is the Law of Attraction and that the "Secret's Secret" is resonance, then we can now define resonance in terms that everyone will be able to grasp. Here we will emphasize the miraculous nature of the biological resonance phenomenon, which is the Secret's Secret.

Resonance is a strong frequency that comes about when the system's natural frequency is stimulated by the same frequency from an outside source.

To understand resonance I will give some physical examples of resonance that will draw attention to the differences between "mechanical resonance" and "biological resonance." We must remember that same-intensity frequencies have the effect of being constructive and stimulating, while a reverse frequency is destructive and disorderly. Data transfer can only take place on frequencies of the same wavelengths. An organism can only receive and comprehend a message on the same frequency. This is exactly the same rationale as radio and television receivers; they can only receive the frequency to which they are tuned.

Every vibration carries data; other energy forms are capable of sending data. Resonance is nothing more than motion that moves backward and forward, up and down.

Resonance is easily seen in a a mechanical apparatus or an electrical circuit. One striking example of resonance concerns the waves from a radio electromagnetic field. The principle of radio and television is based on resonance and the transfer of data on the same wavelength frequency. (As a side note, the inventor of the radio was not Guglielmo Marconi, but Nikola Tesla [1856-1943]. Tesla had achieved this feat prior to Marconi by working on the principle of resonance both as a transmitter and receiver.) This kind of resonance is exactly the same as that found in the human body, which can serve as both a transmitter and a receiver—just like a radio. This is what is called mechanical resonance.

Backward and forward movement is "vibration"; up and down describes oscillation. When an object is resonating the oscillation has a clear and specific frequency. This oscillation can quickly accelerate to become an energy sphere and if the energy is not released it can explode or collapse, whatever the material. The finest example is footage of the destruction of the Tacoma Narrows Bridge in the United States filmed on 7 November, 1940, just four months after it opened. The bridge, designed to withstand winds of up to 140 miles per hour, was destroyed by winds blowing at only 42 miles per hour. As a bridge engineer myself who worked for the New Hampshire Highways Department, I believe this is perhaps the best-known case study of such a phenomenon.

According to conventional wisdom, the bridge's natural vibration or oscillation frequency was designed to withstand winds of up to 140 miles per hour but the potential for low-speed winds from the opposite direction had been overlooked. Because the bridge's natural frequency was the same as that of the 42 mile per hour wind, the bridge began "flapping" up and down and tore itself to pieces before falling into the waters below.

Resonance can thus destroy a bridge with one incorrectly assembled component, just as it can also cause the breakup of a helicopter in mid-air. The destructive characteristics of mechanical resonance should always be considered, as in the Tacoma Narrows Bridge incident, or other serious damage to machinery will occur from time to time. (The effects of mechanical resonance, as seen in the bridge example above, are similar to that of treatments utilizing biological resonance equipment, where the energy blockages in the human organism are removed by disintegrating them.)

If we consider that there are 6.5 billion people living on the planet, then we must imagine them as 6.5 billion radio transmitters and receivers. If this theory is sound and the universe is a network of electromagnetic fields, then everyone is communicating with everyone else without being aware of it. Should you encounter emotional, health or financial problems, you will without exception be in contact with others on the same frequency; you could be helping each other, without anyone knowing. Those searching for love could find love; those searching for healing could find health; those seeking riches could find wealth. All that is required is to be one of those who thinks affirmatively at a high frequency.

## Mechanical Resonance, Biological Resonance and the Resonance of Divine Justice

In general, three conditions are necessary for mechanical resonance to be present. An object must have a natural frequency to resonate. A natural frequency refers to the oscillating capability of a compelled or stimulated object. Oscillation in a mechanical apparatus is characterized by vibration and in an electrical circuit by voltage and flow variation.

The second condition is that the stimulating force must be the same or similar to the object's natural frequency. When the frequency of the force is activated at the same frequency as the object, there is a build-up of energy and, as both are resonating, that energy build up is focused on the object.

The third condition is energy discharge and whether there is a compelling reason for the energy to be discharged.

When homoeopathy and biological resonance are used to correct functional or physical disorders in the body's organism, biological resonance is used as a complete oppositional treatment method. The therapy is used to stimulate the body's defense or immune system. This is a treatment free of pharmaceuticals and in some quarters is regarded as revolutionary. When the immune system is working at full capacity and the body is in holistic equilibrium, there is no illness or condition that cannot be overcome and life can be lived free of ill health with the body becoming ever more resistant to illness.

Resonance is not just confined to health therapies; it is directly concerned with all of our cerebral processes. Returning to the radio illustration, radio stations have a powerful transmitting antenna and the electromagnetic wave frequencies emitted are picked up by tuning our radio receivers into the same frequency. When the resonance phenomenon is achieved we can listen to all the different broadcasts.

If you recall, there are three cornerstones of the universe: energy, matter and information (thought, data, code etc.). As our thoughts become data carrying electromagnetic waves, all that is required is for them to encounter other quantum particles of data vibrating at the same frequency for transmission to occur.

Let us imagine for a moment that, for social or business reasons, we wish to meet or get to know an individual; if we were to turn this thought into a burning desire with sufficient affirmative energy then we become a powerful transmitter with the electromagnetic waves of our thoughts spreading out into the universe. If the other person's thoughts are vibrating and oscillating at the same frequency then resonance will occur and our transmitted energy waves will become "like attracts like," providing an irresistible force for contact to be established. This is the phenomenon of biological resonance.

The manifestation of divine justice is nothing else than the resonance phenomenon. Divine justice means that any wrong or injustice committed against a person or society will one day return to the perpetrator like a boomerang. "You reap what you sow," and "What goes around comes around" are popular descriptions of the phenomenon.

Divine justice represents the Creator's universal justice system. This justice is a manifestation of "the world of cause and effect." Nobody can profit from evil. Those who inflict pain will receive pain. Examples of axioms that define this include "Those who live in glass houses shouldn't throw stones."

Everything in our lives comes at a price that may even be a form of punishment. If we accept the Law of Attraction as an intrinsic part of a divine universe then equally we must accept that divine justice is part of the same system. We can equally apply "like attracts like" to both. Is this not exactly what "good begets good, evil begets evil" means? If divine justice is an aspect of the Law of Attraction then it is a natural conclusion that the resonance phenomenon is a facet of divine justice; therefore, would it not be true to say that it is nothing less than the Secret's Secret itself?

The resonance of divine justice may be characterized as resonant thought that tends to oscillate towards the maximum magnetic frequency capacity. Examples of these could be malevolent or unjust actions, crimes, or other types of cruelty, all of which are expressed by high energy electromagnetic thought waves in the human brain. When we intensely concentrate on negative thought, it is loaded into our brains and realized in an action or thought of the same ilk. The extreme negative energy released by this, in line with the resonance phenomenon, will come back to us in full. We should never dismiss karma, in that every wrong, injustice and hurt we have ever done is stored in our sub-conscious, the "black-box" of our spiritual body if you like, and, through the resonance phenomenon, will return back to us.

We are no different from radio transmitters, whether we are aware of this or not. All our thoughts, affirmative and negative, are continuously vibrating, oscillating particles within the all-embracing energy fields of the endless universe.

Thus, when we transgress, it does not matter if another individual knows for in the divine justice system, reality is much better perceived that we can ever imagine. One way or another, we receive our just retribution.

In the divine justice system the Law of Attraction takes on the properties of three-dimensional resonance, combining the mechanical and biological with its own inimitable divine justice resonance. Mechanical resonance represents the Law of Attraction's destructive role; biological resonance, its healing role; and the divine justice resonance, humanity's and the universe's justice system.

Because they are loaded with energy and broadcasting electromagnetic waves just like a radio transmitter and receiver, our thoughts are phenomenally important in determining the direction our lives take. It all comes down to the Secret being the Law of Attraction and how we have attempted to explain its principles of "like heals like" and "like attracts like." We have emphasized that resonance is the common factor of these two principles and that we must always be in pursuit of constructive, affirmative carrying resonances.

I am utterly convinced that it is only a New Age approach that can only bring us happiness, as well as spiritual, physical and well-being rewards and open up new horizons for the world in which we live.

# IV

# Resonance and Scientific
# Approaches

While Samuel Hanhnemann can be said to be the father of homeopathy as someone who conducted significant research on biological resonance, he is also considered to be a follower of the Isaac Newton school of classical physics.

But while the 21st century continues to appreciate Newton's contribution to macro physics, it is the micro-universe of quantum physics that Albert Einstein's theories introduced, with the resonance phenomenon in particular, that excites today's scientific research. Quantum physics has brought a new dimension to the resonance phenomenon. In recent times, a number of scientists have advanced in their study of the existence of life, with emphasis on human existence in particular. This new understanding has introduced the concept of the universe emerging from a multiverse.

Classical Newtonian physics discusses a whole made up of small components, while quantum physics speaks of a single interactive universe. Humanity is an inseparable part of this whole and is therefore capable of uniting with anything and everything that is in the universe and, through vibration, humans exchange data with every single particle in the universe. This understanding has been given a New Age label but we must remember that the basis of the Law of Attraction is "resonance." The principal of "like attracts like" is a demonstration of resonance; and once again, we can repeat that the Secret's Secret is nothing less than resonance.

In the last ten to fifteen years, major results have been achieved by the scientific research being carried out on biological frequency fields. The most striking of these was published in 1992 and came from the world's first "biological frequency monitor" invented by Bruce Taino. Dr. Robert O. Becker. In his book *The Body Electric,* Becker refers to the relationship between the body's electrical fields and diagnosis in human health and brings our attention to the diagnosis of medical disorders through the utilization of electrical frequency.

In the 1920s, prior to Dr. Becker's work, Dr. Royal Raymond Rife developed a "frequency generator." When used in clinical trials it was able to destroy cancer cells and certain viruses.

Nicola Tesla, the celebrated inventor, conducted studies into how people could be protected from electromagnetic pollution and increase their resistance to illness.

Bruce Taino, working at the independent Taino Technology Department of Eastern State University in Cheny, Washington State, USA, succeeded in establishing the daily norms of healthy body frequencies using his "Frequency Monitor." Taino's clinical trials produced these results:

- The norm for the average adult is a frequency of 62-68 MHz. That is to say, the body magnetically oscillates between 62 and 68 times a second.
- Taino's most important finding was that at a frequency below 62MHz the immune system starts to close down.
- At 58MHz the body is susceptible to common cold viruses and influenza.
- At 55MHz the body becomes susceptible to candiasis (fungal infections).
- At 52MHz the body becomes susceptible to the Epstein Bar virus (herpes) and the immune system becomes threatened.
- At 42MHz an abnormal increase in free radicals occurs with the possibility of tumors forming.

We usually get the flu during the winter months. We are all familiar with the symptoms of headache, runny nose, sore throat and sometimes a high temperature. Even if we take medication it still can last a week or more. But why do we get flu?

Flu viruses are present during a flu epidemic. While the immune system is healthy, that is to say with a dominant bodily frequency of between 62-68 MHz (some researchers set these parameters at 62-78) the virus is suppressed. In a cold ambient environment our frequency falls and when it reaches 58MHz the viruses literally come to life. This is the resonance phenomenon. This is because viruses operate at a 58MHz frequency; when the body falls to the same frequency it creates a resonance condition. Resonance under these circumstances distorts the polarity of the body, causing blockages in the energy flow and empty intervals within the frequency both hindering the defense mechanism and allowing the virus to gain momentum.

Even if the flu virus cannot be destroyed immediately, the swiftest way to overcome it is to generate an oscillating frequency that approximates the virus' own 58MHz, causing the virus to resonate so that "like heals like." This can be achieved with advanced biological resonance apparatus. In addition, the food we consume is an important factor. For example, when we have the flu we must ensure that our diet contains certain foods like red onions. The frequency of red onions is quite similar to that of flu viruses. This is a homeopathic therapy, and as we have mentioned earlier, homeopathy is a resonance phenomenon and the flu virus is a perfect example of the Secret's "like attracts like" and "like heals like," or the Law of Attraction if you prefer.

At the outset, the virus functions in accordance with "like attracts like" by becoming actively threatening. In response, the law of "like heals like" comes into effect with a new resonance making the flu virus impotent.

One of the most exciting areas of research conducted on

bodily frequency ranges has been cellular metabolism. As with all living organisms, our bodies have measurable frequency ranges of vibration and oscillation. Research observes that every medical disorder has its own signature at clearly defined ranges of different frequencies. This work has opened up a new dimension in diagnosis using frequency monitors and or biological resonance equipment.

One of the most important findings from this research has been that while infected cells show clear evidence of being sensitive to small frequency ranges, healthy cells show no reaction at all. According to this research the dominant bodily frequency of a healthy person should average between 62-78. The subtle bodies oscillate between 70-78 million times per second while the oscillation repetition is between 62-70MHz in the physical body. The frequency range at the cellular level is between 62-72MHz and, for example, when infection with the common cold is present, it can fall as low as 58Mhz. As a reminder, 1 Hertz (Hz) is one oscillation per second while a Megahertz (MHz) is a million. The dominant or basic resonance frequency of our bodies are in a clearly defined threshold range which, as a result of vibration, also shows an oscillation measurement of 58MHz in the case of the common cold. This threshold range is the limit of bodily defense.

The resonance understanding of the cause of headaches is that they are energy blockages; energy blockages are destructive and as a result the brain and nervous system stimulate the immune system to counter this and eliminate the symptoms of the headache.

## Homeopathy and Biological Resonance

We should mention here that—to complement to our physical bodies—we all possess a holographic energy model that can be characterized as the etheric body. Research has revealed that even preceding the physical signs of a medical disorder, the problem can be clearly observed in the etheric body. Thus we can see that illness and even cellular changes first start at the etheric bodily level.

Immune system failure against infection or serious conditions such as cancer can partly be attributed to weakness in anticipated energy levels. Kirlian photography and similar diagnostic methods demonstrate the prescient diagnosis of potential medical conditions.

If we accept the theory that the first indications of health disorders are to be seen in the etheric body, is it possible to consider commencing treatment at this level? Research has shown that this farsighted approach could be a possible treatment option, whereby the etheric patterns are corrected, thus curing what would have been eventually a physical condition.

While MRI (Magnetic Resonance Imaging) is still considered one of the foremost weapons in the armory of orthodox diagnosis, it is really no more than a sophisticated piece of Newtonian equipment and in the near future when Kirlian photography is combined with MRI technology there will be a new chapter opened in the history of early diagnosis. Similarly, the static technology of MRI has already been superseded by the dynamic technology of fMRI (Functional Magnetic Resonance Imaging). While imaging a part of the anatomy, the brain for example, fMRI can measure the cerebral blood flow, its volume and oxygen level at the same time. fMRI can deliver a three dimensional image by stimulating the protons of the cells. This machine could, at the same time, be considered to be the first holographic apparatus.

Holography is the process of producing a three-dimensional image using lasers. The etymology is once again ancient Greek; from 'holos' (whole) and 'graphe' (writing or drawing). A hologram is the three-dimensional representation of an actual object. This technology is still in its infancy, however in association with Kirlian photography there exists the possibility of introducing an exciting new age in early diagnosis. To offer a simple example, a nominally healthy individual's dominant energy frequency resonates at a value of 65Hz. If this individual is infected by a pathogenic bacterium he or she will probably display symptoms of fever and shivering. In terms of cellular physiology, fever can be a positive reaction in bacterial infections. The body's defense mechanism employs higher than normal temperatures as they are shown to destroy bacteria. From an energy point of view, the common cold victim will display a frequency different to 65Hz, 58Hz for example. The immune system must generate in excess of this for the virus to overcome 62 and for the return to health. If the individual wishes to speed up this process and is skeptical of allopathic medication with its unknown side effects, treatment options can include homeopathic remedies or biological frequency equipment to stimulate the defense mechanism.

It is striking that in modern allopathic treatment a multi-medication "cocktail" approach is prevalent, whereas homeopathy is based on getting results with just one, specific condition-orientated, preparation. The holistic treatment of the patient is achieved by stimulating the immune mechanism with the one preparation in homeopathy or by using biological frequency equipment. Both treatments can be used at the same time as they complement each other.

Treatment using the "resonance" phenomenon is not just confined to physical disorders; emotional and psychological conditions can also be treated. It is essential that the correct vibrational frequency is matched to the patient's condition. As result of this broad spectrum approach involving the patient's physical, emotional, mental and spiritual well-being, it can be considered medicine's first truly holistic approach. The philosophical difference between the two approaches is most evident in the example used above, the multi-medication approach to treating the common cold attempts to cure at the cellular level whereas with just a single homeopathic preparation, the treatment is achieved by stimulating the energy level.

Some sources consider homeopathic remedies "physical" because of the direct energy effect they have at the molecular level. The effects that homeopathic remedies have on both the etheric and physical body in Kirlian and other electrographic techniques are observable.

While pharmacologists isolate the active molecules of plants to produce synthetic drugs, in homeopathy the entire plant or matter is used so as to take advantage of its vibrationary properties. The energy properties of the plant are absorbed by the water in which homeopathic remedies are prepared; they are dispensed in the form and dosage suitable for each patient. In this sense homeopathic remedies can be characterized as etheric remedies. The water retains an imprint of the properties of the plant or matter as well as a blueprint of its physical molecular structure; these are broken down (by dilution) into the energy or etheric properties and the imprint of these properties is passed onto the etheric body. This is why the more the preparation is diluted, the more its homeopathic effectiveness increases.

Let us consider for a moment how the dilution process functions and how efficacy increases in "homeopathic" remedies. For example, when we ingest a plant or herb that affects the organelle of a cell in the physical body, it must first pass through the digestive system and the right conditions must exist in the intestines for it to be absorbed and for the toxic matter to be separated from active ingredient and for this, the matrix or connective tissue must be both conductive and functioning. In addition, the cells must be functioning well and able to absorb and use the active material.

On the contrary, when a homeopathic remedy is used, the remedy already contains the data on the active ingredient of the plant that has been maximized by dilution. These data are transmitted directly to the etheric body and from there the correctly coded stimulus is sent directly to the cells in the physical body. In a homeopathic preparation, the smaller the molecular trace, the greater its efficacy. With its projected effect in mind, when homeopathic remedies are prepared, the therapeutic characteristics of a plant's flowers and leaves are considered separate entities. Different parts of the same plant have different energy properties, all of which support this hypothesis.

Herbal treatments have a far wider acceptance than conventional remedies because they rely on Newtonian medicine where the molecule is the active agent. Understanding the efficacy of homeopathic remedies depends on the observation of the patient and their health situation with relation to their energy levels

Orthodox medicine, limited by the conventional pathophysiological model, leaves many physicians unable to comprehend how treatments with micro-doses of a substance can be successful. In the final analysis, no one can deny the efficacy of orthodox medicine for intervention at the acute stage of immune related disorders. What I have tried to demonstrate here is that the homeopathic and biological resonance approach can be complementary to orthodox medicine in the treatment of chronic debilitating illnesses.

## The Emoto Magnetic Resonance Analyzer

Masaru Emoto is a renowned researcher and writer; his books have now been translated into English and many have had a chance to read and investigate his ideas. While writing this book about resonance, I discovered that Masuro Emoto is one of the best sources for demonstrating the wider implications of resonance.

At 43 years old, Emoto began his research using low frequency medical therapy equipment. After an introduction to an American doctor, Lee H. Lorenzen, the two men collaborated on developing equipment to measure the quality of water. On the recommendation of Dr. Lorenzen they began to use in their experiments a Bio-Cellular Analyzer invented by Roland J. Weinstock. While Dr. Lorenzen had previously been using equipment that could measure quantity, Weinstock's apparatus could measure water quality. In addition to its use for measuring water quality, this apparatus was also being frequently used in the preparation of homeopathic remedies.

Emoto purchased three of these devices and returned to

Japan. The correct name of this machine is Magnetic Resonance Analyzer or MRA. An important function of the MRA is to detect and record imbalanced resonance. Emoto called this process "HADO," meaning "wave movement." Working from the Lorenzen-designed water micro-clusters, Emoto developed HADO water. Water micro-clusters are reconstituted water that reveal their micro-water properties. After removing acidic elements from the water, the equipment reconstitutes it in its alkali and ionized micro-water form. HADO water is, for all intents and purposes, a homeopathic preparation. At that period in Japan prohibitions against practicing homeopathy without a doctor's license were being enforced, so Emoto was unable to give his water diluted in alcohol a homeopathic title.

From 1987 to 1994, Emoto worked as a healer, with his homeopathic HADO water affecting many near-miraculous cures. To introduce a wider public to his work he wrote several books, among the most popular are: *The Hidden Messages in Water, Messages from the Water and Universe,* and *Water Crystal Healing: Music and Images to Restore Your Well-Being.*

In his book, *Love Thyself,* Masuro Emoto explains HADO, saying that it is nothing more than a resonance phenomenon. We have emphasized that energy is a vibration, the result of which is that life can only be sustained by life's vibration, and the best example of that is "a heart that does not vibrate is dead."

While accepting that the resonance phenomenon is the system of uninterrupted vibration with sympathetic vibration of comparative frequencies let us attempt to illustrate with tuning fork examples. Imagine three tuning forks: two are tuned to the same frequency of 440Hz and the third to 442Hz. If we strike the 440Hz tuning fork and hold it near the one of the same Hz we will immediately hear and see it vibrating in harmony. But if we try the same by striking the 442Hz tuning fork we will see no response in the other two.

Emoto's hypothesis for HADO water can be sustained in

this way: the vibration of the energy in the preparation is the same as that of the patient so that a resonance is brought into play, thereby curing the disorder. As previously mentioned, Emoto's methods can be accepted as standard homeopathic practice.

Among the most important of Emoto's efforts is his pioneering work in photographing ice crystals. His original intention in doing this was to photographically record and compare HADO water before and after vibrational duplication. In this way he hoped to prove that homeopathy's efficacy was a result of the resonance phenomenon and the type of healing role it played would be recorded in the ice crystal. In 1994 Emoto succeeded in producing the first images of ice crystals in the laboratory conditions of his own lab. Here was concrete evidence of the resonance phenomenon for all to see.

These photographs proved to be both proof of the resonance phenomenon and concrete evidence of the extraordinary power of the mind and thought. People were astonished by the extraordinary beauty of the before and after photographs of ice crystals that had received directed affirmative thought or prayers.

Most surprising of all is that so many people have - for whatever reason and without examining the scientific explanations - begun to accept this phenomenon. I do not understand why, when the Law of Attraction exists with "like attracts like", with thought and senses having a physical outcome, why looking at some photographs of the changes imposed on water enables individuals to unconditionally accept all. Of course, when we can see physical evidence of a miraculous phenomenon we are immediately inclined to accept it; but without researching the reasons behind anything, how can we consider ourselves to possess all the facts?

Masuro Emoto succeeded in showing us through pictures how our health can be augmented by the power of affirmative thought. But researchers with a sensitivity and interest in the reality of how thought affects the physical reality missed the point of what Emoto was trying to prove. In the course of our research we have discovered very few commentators who have actually discussed the real purpose of his research and philosophy.

The most effective way is to listen to the man himself and so I include a paraphrase from his book *Love Thyself*, where he reminds us that each and every snowflake is different. He expanded this to include frozen water and learned that when he did freeze water, each ice crystal is unique.

Hado photographed the ice crystals before and after they had been loaded with HADO (vibrational) data and in this way showed the extraordinary differences that occurred, thus leading to a wider acceptance of the existence of HADO. He says that he felt completely vindicated when he saw this had been turned into reality.

As noted in the sections on homeopathy and biological resonance, HADO, or in homeopathic remedies, the plant or material's energy data, are imprinted in the water, which is then used as individual doses. This is the same process that Emoto explains when he refers to HADO vibrations. In the same book, Emoto refers to how his journey started with the Magnetic Resonance Analyzer that he used at the beginning of his research. It is a strange coincidence, but the secret of the Law of Attraction is resonance and we find that we are confronted with the philosophy behind HADO as being resonance itself.

When it comes to how we can positively affect our health with just affirmative thought, this is a subject on which we will go into greater detail in the "What We Must Do for the Health of Our Bodies" chapter.

It is no coincidence that what we have been doing is to explain how we must live energy-filled lives and how this can affect our well-being. Emoto reveals it in exactly the same way.

Many researchers have confirmed this by using the description: "Water changes its own appearance." But the whys and wherefores of its changes are a mystery I would like to spend a little more time examining. Likewise, to those whose interest has been roused by "water" and wish to read more, I strongly recommend Dr. F.Batmanghelidj's book: *You Are Not Sick, You ARE Thirsty! For Health, For Healing, For LIFE.*

Picture caption page 82/1) Frozen crystal of Zamzam water
(Source: *Love Thyself*, Masaru Emoto)

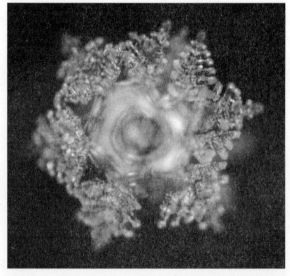

Picture caption page 82/2) A frozen water crystal that
has been resonated (Source: *Love Thyself*, Masaru Emoto)

Picture caption page 83) A frozen water crystal from the faucet before prayer. (Source: *Love Thyself*, Masaru Emoto)

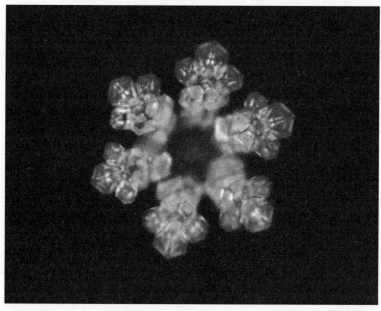

(Picture caption page 84) A frozen water crystal from the faucet after prayer. (Source: *Love Thyself*, Masaru Emoto)

# Resonance Repatterning (RR) and the Bi-Digital O Ring

Chloe Wordsworth was one of the pioneers of "Resonance Repatterning." In her book, *Quantum Change Made Easy*, she brought a fresh perspective to the resonance approach. Initially this concept was called "Holographic Repatterning," later modified to "Resonance Repatterning." The concept describes the process of cleansing our convictions, behavior, thoughts and feelings of the negativity that restricts the way we live our lives. These restrictions can prevent us from leading a healthy, happy life. The patterns of these restrictions begin from our childhood years and eventually may form a barrier around our subconscious that can be an obstacle for the rest of our lives. These subconscious patterns or molds relentlessly block our aspirations for happiness, health, love and wealth. These barriers exist beyond our normal conscious awareness and as long as we fail to find the reasons behind these issues we are condemned to a life of unhappiness. What "Resonance Repatterning," which we will refer to as "RR," attempts to do is move the negativity within our subconscious to a conscious level. Chloe Wordsworth developed a method for this more than 25 years ago. In order for individuals to be in a state of what is called "consistency," or balanced and well adjusted, she proposed a holographic map to indicate the barriers that must be removed. This could be achieved using Kinesiology methods.

According to available documentation, the term Kinesiology was first used in 1857 by Dally in his book *Cinesiologie ou Science du Mouvement*. Dally studied the science of human movement, something that has been developed even further with the Kinesiology method, all of which have excited great interest. The method uses the body's bio-feedback system and examines, diagnoses and records the sensitive relationship between the muscle physiology and the internal organs of the bodily system.

The complementary methods that can be used to rebalance and readjust the body are:

- Spinal Reflex System
- Neuro-Emotional System
- Neuro-Lymphatic System
- Acu-points
- Meridian Energy Flow
- Neuro-Vascular system
- Emotional Stress Release
- Flower Essences and Homeopathic Remedies
- Nutritional Support
- Lifestyle Improvements, Exercise etc.

According to "RR," which has been developed from the principles of resonance, everything is in a condition of vibration and when these vibrations are at the same frequency, there is a state of resonance. When we are in resonance, when our vital connections and associated probabilities have been corrected, all barriers are eliminated from our bodies due to the increased energy that now envelopes us. If we are in resonance with a discrete thing or individual, we will be able to feel and experience it.

Dr. Yashiaki Omura is an eminent scientist who conducted important work on Kinesiology. Dr. Omura's contribution has been the development of the Bio-Digital O Ring test (BDORT), an application of Kinesiology that is an important facet of complementary medicine.

Dr. Omura's test is conducted with the patient making an "O" with the thumb and forefinger of one hand while (for instance) touching a scar on their body with the forefinger of the other hand. The practitioner attempts to pry apart the patient's two fingers by using both their hands, also held in the

"O" shape position. In this example, the patient's fingers separate immediately because the energy flow is hindered in the part of the body where there is scar tissue, thus limiting the body's general energy potential. The patient is then directed to touch a healthy part of the body. Now it becomes difficult or near impossible to separate the patients "O" formed fingers as they have full resistance. (I was the patient in the example, and the practitioner a physician friend who had completed his training in Germany).

This method is not just limited to this example; the same methodology can achieve a wide range of diagnostic results. Among these is the Dysfunction Localization Method that can diagnose malfunctioning organs. Another is the Drug Compatibility Test. The drug in question is placed in the palm of the patient's other hand and the result reveals whether the aforementioned drug is suitable for the patient. There are more examples; but in order not to deviate from the subject, I will not mention them here.

One of the "BDORT's most interesting and persuasive aspects is that my physian friend used exactly the same procedure to test my thoughts.

When I thought about something in a negative way, my fingers easily separated from their "O" shape; however when I considered something affirmatively I surprised myself with the strength and resistance in my fingers. This brief demonstration just shows how negative thought or, for want of a better word, stress, saps the energy from our bodies.

Dr. Omura's scientific findings are an important contribution to the subject here for the "BDORT" method uses the Resonance Phenomenon on the points of the body that represent the internal organs and, by observing differences in the muscle strength, can reach a highly accurate diagnosis. The introduction of a new example of resonance only proves, once again, how broad its field of application really is.

# Morphic Resonance

Dr. Rupert Sheldrake is a celebrated research biologist known for his scientific research into the structure of biology and the physical reality. His work has brought a new view and approach to Darwin's theories on evolution.

Sheldrake devised the concept of the "Morphic field," proposing that in addition to the energy and material factors of every system, there are also other organized invisible and intangible fields. He calls these "Morphic Fields."

While proposing a form to these morphic fields he also suggested that there were particles that made up these fields. He called these particles "morphic units." According to Sheldrake's premise, morphic fields are formed from morphic units that come into being from collective behavior and/or collective thought. The hypothesis is that a particular form belonging to a certain group with an already established collective morphic field will tune into that morphic field. Thus the morphic field's database gains a new dimension.

Over time and with the participation of new forms, the morphic field becomes stronger while at the same time those of the same species can have a reciprocal influence within the morphic field. If there is repetitive behavior among a species for long enough, "Morphic Resonance" may affect the rest of the species.

The basis of the Sheldrake Model is the hypothesis of morphic resonance. He explains morphic resonance as a feedback mechanism between the morphic field and the morphic units. The greater the degree of similarity, the greater the resonance, leading to habituation or persistence of particular forms. The existence of a morphic field makes it far easier for the existence of a new similar form.

In Rupert Sheldrake's book, *A New Science of Life*, he presented his findings from experiments with mice to back up his hypothesis of "Morphic Resonance," creating, in the process, almost as great a stir as Darwin did with his theories on evolution:

Under laboratory conditions the collective intelligence of mice that had learned their way around a maze was observed to facilitate the ease with which a separate group of mice learned their way around an identical maze in another laboratory. From this evidence Sheldrake devised the term "morphic resonance." According to the hypothesis, an organism is directly affected by former behavior and form, whether it is human, animal or plant. As in the experiment, when one group of mice learns something, another separate group of mice can benefit from this knowledge. This is an event that Sheldrake defined as a "morphogenetic field" when the field is an active mode and has the capability of "remote effect." The etymology of the word is 'morphos', form, and 'genesis', creation; the application here describes the way in which tissue, organs and all life are given form by certain governing principles. Morphogenetic fields are defined by Sheldrake as the subset of morphic fields which influence, and are influenced by, living things.

Morphogenetic fields contain the definitive data for development from the embryonic stage; the egg and sperm are also data carriers. All information for giving life a form is concealed within the morphogenetic field. There are three components that make up the morphic field. These are the morphogenetic field, the sub-quantum field and the potential field. Morphic resonance constitutes the lines of communication between the connected and related forms.

We find another example of morphic resonance mentioned in Law Watson's book *Lifedite*. Watson has conducted research similar to Sheldrake's, has made similar observations, and also supports the "morphic resonance" argument. Watson gives an example of the same species of monkey living on different islands of an archipelago. When the monkeys on one island develop new behavioral patterns it spreads to the other monkeys and yet the monkeys cannot communicate between the islands. Watson attributes this to "morphic resonance."

It might not seem reasonable for us to be convinced by the morphic field only by studying Rupert Sheldrake's hypothesis;

but experiments commenced in 1998 at the Princeton Engineering Anomalies Research Lab (PEAR) have provided serious evidence for the probability of morphic fields. The laboratory devised a system whereby diodes were placed in different zones around the world; the white noise emitted by the diodes was evaluated by a web hosted by fifty computers in the lab. Each morning the raw data of white sound were transmitted to the diodes and the responses were recorded by the computers. Over a period of time, findings indicated that the responses were synchronized with the most important human events happening in the world at that particular moment and indicated that the diodes were affected by these events. The most surprising findings were that the diodes showed high activity hours before the attacks on the Twin Towers of 9/11 and the subsequent invasion of Iraq. Data indicated that the global consciousness recorded high activity as relayed by the diodes five hours before the first plane crashed into the towers at 8.45, and six hours before the second plane crashed at 10.30.

The plane hijackers and the terrorist organization that planned the attack acted like a radio transmitters on the morphic field frequencies with both the subconscious of the global consciousness and the diodes tuning into this all around the world. The existence of morphic fields thus clearly demonstrates that because of our extrasensory sub-conscious perception as indicated in the morphic fields, we are inextricably joined to each other. Once again we see how scientific research reveals how resonance is an enigmatic and compelling a cosmic force.

Many people may find this difficult to accept, but for further convincing I suggest they check the Princeton University website and read more about these findings.

## Schumann Resonance

Schumann Resonance is found between the surface of the earth and ozone layer in the dense ionosphere and is on an extremely low frequency (ELF) electromagnetic wave length.

This resonance has a value of 7.83Hz and is the resonance of the planet itself. Its fluctuation between ± 0.5Hz is caused by the solar winds that are created in the nuclear reactions of the sun that turn hydrogen into helium.

Although "Schumann Resonance" is an accepted scientific reality, there are few scientists who understand its significance in the equilibrium of life or as the frequency of life's tuning fork. Schumann Resonance is closely related to the direct health of the individual. Any frequency outside this wavelength has a detrimental and health-threatening effect for all mammals on the brain's biological oscillator. This is because the brain's vibratory frequency is the same as that of the planet. The brain's frequency is sometimes called the Alpha Rhythm and this and the earth both have a frequency of 7.83Hz.

Dr. Wolfgang Ludwig wrote a paper on the effects of the Schumann frequency with reference to healthy environmental conditions by taking readings from both the surface of the planet and underground. During his research he discovered that perfect health in humans required the same frequency in both places. Dr. Ludwig published his studies in his book, *Informative Medizin*, and suggested the serious health dangers to those who are getting only one of these wavelengths, for instance, underground workers like miners. Dr Ludwig also noted that astronauts and cosmonauts face the same hazards when they leave the earth's magnetic field. In 1974 equipment was developed for use in spacecraft to act as a frequency regulator. There still remains further serious scientific research to be conducted into the "devastating" effect of the Schumann resonance phenomenon, particularly now that the risks it poses to human health have been exposed.

The threats inherent in wireless communication, microwave technology and cell phone radiation threat to our health have also emerged and the current environmental conditions in which we live indicate we are moving towards a completely unsynchronized relationship with nature. This is why we must all be fully aware of the importance of Schumann resonance and make ourselves heard, so that necessary technical precautions can be taken as soon as possible to avoid the countless dangers that this poses to our health.

To summarize, Schumann resonance is, just like biological resonance, another aspect of the resonance phenomenon that impacts our health.

## Infoseuticals and Biological Resonance

In his book, *Decoding the Human Body Field*, Prof. Peter H. Fraser talks of the growing paradigm in the fields of biology and medicine. Prof. Fraser published his book in 2008 and defined this new paradigm in biology and medicine:

> Our bodies are subjected to many influences outside of the normal biochemical set up. Whether the causes are emotional or physical, we have a pressing need to overcome their symptoms. The real reasons for these disorders are revealed at the sub-cellular level with the energy and physiological data of quantum waves, forces, and fields. At this level our very thoughts and beliefs affect our health.
>
> Scientific research has proven that our cells, organs and immune system are directly affected by thoughts, beliefs, emotions and behavior. It is of the paramount that we are aware of the undeniable fact that non-physical effects such as our thoughts, beliefs, expectations and desires can all change our body chemistry.
>
> When we descend into the sub-atomic world it is not just the rules of chemistry that are in control, we also observe that the quantum electro-dynamic challenges all the accepted principles.

Scientists have discovered that the body has the ability to possess a holographic composition with cells radiating on a clearly defined wavelength; as the nervous system is made up of neurons and synapses, there is something comparable to a secondary nervous system which is an advanced data network system storing information about our muscles while our body fluids too, have the ability to store and transport data.

I have mentioned how conventional pharmaceuticals are produced by isolating the active ingredients from organic or inorganic sources to make drugs; I have also discussed their differences with homeopathy, where the vibrational frequencies of organic or inorganic material are used to create remedies. But there is a third and new medicinal option; this option is activated or energized medication called infoseuticals. These remedies are preparations that have been loaded with condition-relevant data.

While homeopathic remedies retain the energy characteristics of the organic or inorganic material from which they have been prepared in highly diluted form, infoseuticals have energy data, in the form of vibration or oscillation measured in Hertz, loaded into the water medium by defined methods or using special equipment. Infoseuticals are not chemical, herbal or food supplement pharmaceuticals; neither are they homeopathic or herbal remedies, but are, rather, micro-measured colloidal mineral preparations. The minerals at the sub-atomic level carry codes pertaining to the human body field. Programmed infoseuticals are devised to directly treat the body field. The result of the treatment is to remove or disintegrate the blockages that occur after shock, trauma, toxic accumulation or psychological disorders. Thus the immune system can be empowered to heal from within.

Prof. Peter H. Fraser heads an organization that currently commercially produces 62 infoceutical preparations that can be grouped into five different categories.

**Big Field Aligners**: These preparations have been designed to treat disorders in misalignment of the human body field with the natural gravitational and magnetic polar fields.

**Energetic Drivers**: These energize the body field so that detoxification can commence and stimulate the activity levels of the organs.

**Energetic Integrators:** These integrators interact with acupuncture meridians correcting mental functions and emotional communication.

**Energetic Terrains**: These are used to support tissue and energetic disturbances cleansing.

**Energetic Stars:** These are used in the treatment of major blockages in the body's metabolic pathways and survival systems.

The preparations are in drop form and prescribed by practitioners. While they do resemble homeopathic remedies, they are a more sophisticated method of treatment directed precisely at the human body-field. The new treatment option of infoseuticals is, as with homeopathic remedies, based on the resonance phenomenon, but this time with a completely new approach.

# V

# Vibrational Medicine
# (Bio-Informational Medicine)

Vibrational medicine or as I call it Bio-Informational Medicine[*], is a body of entirely new treatment methods based on the Einstein paradigm. Einstein's celebrated formula for the theory of relativity, $E=MC^2$, has opened up new horizons for science and gained new perspectives by accepting that energy and matter are just two concepts explaining the reality of the same universe. Based on this paradigm, this new form of medicine acts as a bridge between conventional and complementary medicine and can be described as an application made up of the complex energy fields that perform as a network connecting the body's physical and cellular systems to each other.

The clinical approach of vibrational medicine rests on regulating the energy levels in their own individual energy forms and thus healing the disorders that have arisen from the system's balance being impeded. This may be characterized as the restructuring of cellular physiology by balancing the energy fields so as to put the bodily functions in order and forward the process of healing.

Universal reality can be defined as the basic energy or vibration characteristic that is common to all of us. Vibrational medicine thus becomes the healing practice of manipulating or

[*] My know-how derives from my medical company, which initiated the first bio-informational medicine polyclinic in Turkey.

stimulating the body at the basic vibrational level. The Einstein approach contrasts with conventional medicine, which can be described as having a Newtonian approach. If we were to use the analogy of plumbers and electro-technicians we could describe the approach of Newtonian medicine to resemble that of bio-plumbers while that of the medicine of Einstein can be said to resemble bio-electro-technicians.

In traditional medical approaches the patient's physiological and psychological conditions are approached as if they are computer software. There are still many physicians who see the human body as no more than a complex piece of machinery and there are very few imaginative physicians who can examine the biological circuit board at the molecular level. The starting point of much of Newtonian medicine is surgical intervention. The first surgeons regarded the human body as something similar to a complex plumbing system to be repaired.

Advances in pharmacology then gave rise to the development of a second alternative method based on attempts to repair the disorders in our bodies. Despite being two different schools of thought, they are remarkably similar in that treatment by medication regards the organs of the body, the enzymes and receptors as nothing more than a complex bio-mechanism.

Despite these approaches we know that the human body is far more advanced than a chemical reaction driven machine. Our bodies have a basic life force that exists at a very low frequency in all organisms and that maintains molecular form, synergy and the advancement of all the life functions. At death, this life force leaves the body and it is at that point that the corpse becomes a physical mechanism rapidly moving into decay. This is the most important principal separating animate and inanimate systems and the human being and machines and this is also why the human body should never be considered as merely a collection of cells.

In his book *The Body Electric*, Dr. Robert O. Becker, known for his innovative research, made important breakthroughs by discovering that through the use of electrographic equipment the body can be stimulated so that the capability for tissue renewal can be increased and that the electrical current in the nervous system aided in the repair and regeneration of tissue. The body's electrical system thus plays an important role in vibrational medicine.

Unlike conventional pharmaceuticals and surgery, vibrational medicine aims to cure the patient with pure energy. The physical body includes a low frequency hierarchical energy system that coordinates its electrophysiological and hormonal functions. In situations of health, but also in serious ill health, high energy build-ups are formed in the etheric body. The individual's energy system is highly influenced by nutritional and environmental factors, as well as by their emotional and metaphysical balance. Metaphysical energy is the life force of the bodily structure. This invisible link between the physical body and metaphysical energy is our key to helping us understand the relationship between matter and energy.

Vibrational medicine utilizes an electro-biofeedback procedure that is based on putting the patient's internal frequencies into order. This is called *System Information Therapy (SIT)* or sometimes *Bio-resonance Therapy*. The focus frequency of the disorder in the body is ascertained and corrected with diagnostic equipment by sending stimulating pulses to the patient so that they have the ability to heal themselves. This is the fundamental basis of the "resonance" phenomenon.

The organism has the power to decipher the required vibrational data and to trigger the body into stimulating the necessary repairs. Such is the strength of this conviction that there is no therapy that exists in orthodox medicine that displays such practicality and effectiveness. The application of this theory, however, requires an extraordinary amount of electronic and information technology.

The data required for a successful application of this method are bipolar with a low level of current. The use of pre-programmed stages has allowed the practitioner to gain time in daily applications and has made such therapy both more secure and easier to apply. The method, apart from anything else, is a potent magnetic field therapy. As a treatment it has particularly demonstrated astonishing speed and efficacy in reducing pain. In the course of the therapy the therapist can prepare harmonized vibrations without interrupting the treatment. In this way, different effects can be examined and important data collected so that the appropriate complementary formulations can be prepared (e.g. homeopathic remedies, Bach Flower remedies, nosodes, detoxificants etc.)

Let's now examine these methods in more detail:

Bach Flower Therapy is the therapy choice for non-physical disorders including those with psychological or emotional origins. The vibrational frequencies of wild flowers and vegetable matter are used to treat and stimulate the energy blockages that have occurred as a result of emotional problems.

The affirmative energy vibrations penetrate the body and aid the patient in developing a positive mental outlook. First, the therapist has a pre-therapy session with the patient and the correct flowers for the patient's treatment are selected with the aid of illustrations. Once the remedies have been prepared, they are prescribed for the patient's use. However, this form of therapy can now be accomplished just by using biological resonance equipment.

When the homeopathic remedies or nosodes have been prepared from vegetable or organic material they are stored in glass containers and, as they are in German pharmacies, sold for the use of therapists. To treat disorders like stress, depression and extreme melancholy, the therapist refers to the instrument's menu and prepares a suitable program by selecting an appropriate remedy that is then positioned in a special compartment and thus the instrument can be focused on that specific disorder. With the vibrational frequencies of the remedies and the corresponding electromagnetic stimulus given by the instrument and the resonance phenomenon that results, it is possible to regulate the body's imbalances.

Detoxification formulas use the second method that I have had occasion to refer to before, namely "inversion"; this can be applied by the instrument for regulating and neutralizing disorders and removing them from the body. The same method can be used for addiction therapies such as for cigarettes and alcohol.

The principles of electro-biofeedback equipment can be summed up in the following way: At the heart of the apparatus is the IFS or Individual Frequency Store. The IFS records the patient's internal vibration with two silver bipolar electrodes and stores the data in the paramagnetic biological system. The patient's vibrational data is readjusted and then retransmitted back to the patient by means of a second bipolar circuit from the storage unit of the apparatus, thus boosting the immune system and integrating the healing process.

Combination therapies are those where the patient's internal vibrations are combined with the electronic impulses produced from the biological resonance equipment and various carefully selected and evolved materials such as precious stones, medications or homeopathic remedies. Here, the multidirectional effects are amplified using magnetic screens. The equipment can, with the assistance of these screens and the data collected from the evaluated materials, be combined to treat the patient.

In the case of Magnetic Field Therapy, pulsating magnetic fields are, from a biological point of view, highly effective. Clinical trials have won the acceptance of orthodox practitioners as well, for with this therapy pain is reduced almost instantaneously with a combination of the equipment's support impulses, the stored vibrational information on the disorder and the material's data, together creating potent magnetic fields. This biological technique has been able to greatly enhance the speed at which cellular function related disorders are returned to good health.

Another piece of equipment uses vibrational medicine to synergistically combine three therapies simultaneously. This device is used for treating deterioration and detoxification of the soft connective tissue that is also called the matrix, which is the nutritional and cleansing system of the cells of the bodily organs.

The matrix plays an important role in typical degenerative disorders that have become so prevalent. This is because excess acid, chronic inflammation and infection, pollution, poor diet, stress and general unhealthy conditions continually strain the matrix and negatively effect the nutrition of the organs' cellular system.

The matrix connects the circulatory, nervous and lymphatic systems and is, in effect, the essential infra-structure that provides nutrition to the cellular system of the organs. The ability of the matrix to function becomes limited by the build-up of toxins so the result can only be illness. When this situation occurs, medication or other forms of conventional treatment are unable to reach the organ's affected cells by way of the matrix.

The vibrational medicine equipment we have already referred to treats these types of cases where there is an excessive negative load and build-up of acid by giving a weak corrective current, thus neutralizing the negative load and bringing the tissue back to its correct pH alkali level so that the metabolic functions can return to normal. The same equipment can, while simultaneously combined with a petechial absorption massage, bring waste material and toxins to the surface enabling absorption and elimination from the body by the lymphatic system. The equipment's other synergic therapy is the biological resonance process similar to that used in SIT, System Information Therapy. In this process the cell system, cleansed of the toxins and waste matter in the matrix and thanks to a regained healthy metabolism, can actually increase its energy level. Thus the ability for the body to heal itself is activated and the burden taken off the body's immune system.

When scientists discover the real relationship between matter, energy and information, then they will be that much closer to understanding the link between humanity and the divine.

Vibrational medicine is the scientific approach of the future simply because physicians will eventually be able to understand why one group of people is in good health and another in poor, when they both appear to share the same environment and conditions. Only when the relationship between psychological, emotional, metaphysical and physical health and the universal laws that govern them are understood, can there be a truly holistic approach to medicine.

But while we see all the potentials inherent in vibrational medicine it should be emphasized that we should never completely reject all the possibilities and practices of orthodox Newtonian medicine; on the contrary they should and must be utilized as well; the ideal is that, with an Einstein-like approach that encapsulates vibrational medicine, we should strive for an integration of all disciplines to meet the needs of the patient. The goal is, quite simply, to strengthen the immune system of the patient so that the illness can be overcome from within.

## The body's data-energy fields

The chemical processes that occur in our bodies can, in fact, be best described as bio-physical processes. These come about from a transfer of electrons in the molecule concerned, that is, in the form of pure energy. Not surprisingly, we have now entered the domain of quantum physics.

For all the myriads of processes that occur in the body to be accomplished correctly, all the necessary information must be transmitted rapidly and accurately. What we can take from this is that there cannot be one metabolic reaction taking place in the body that has not received the correct information or instructions to do so. This is the starting point for the rationale behind system information therapy.

Three basic principals differentiate the animate from the inanimate. These are: an "electric current" providing the cells' energy load, "information transfer" governing and directing all the body's processes, and finally, the "metaphysical component" that provides stimulation. There is no more succinct guide than this for our body's bio-chemistry which is why, with this approach, new thresholds of medicine are inescapable. Our bodies are not some mechanical automated random system; the data are profound and the reality multidimensional and must be always regarded as a complex system close to perfection. This does not mean that all classical approaches are wrong, only that the perspectives have irreversibly changed and that the simplistic "either-or" approach to diagnosis has changed to a multi-causal approachwhere a holistic approach dominates.

Disorders evolve from more than one source and must be treated accordingly. Classical or orthodox medicine's most successful advances have been in exigency interventions such as A&E, intensive care, surgery and anesthetics and cardiology; however, the same level of success has not been achieved in the treatment of chronic illness. It is even the case that because they block the functions of the organs, the treatment of disorders with medication such as antibiotics, anti-inflammatory drugs and anti-pyretics sometimes actually have a detrimental rather than a beneficial effect.

As three quarters of all illnesses are chronic disorders, the seriousness of the situation is clear for all to see. The remaining quarter can, even if treated, when augmented with stress, poor diet etc., easily become chronic disorders as well. This only goes to emphasize the importance of the new approaches.

One of the standbys of the new procedures is SIT, System Information Therapy. As we have noted before, this therapy system bases its treatment on "biological resonance." At this point we should to touch on the quantum dimension of this therapy.

The essential way to characterize SIT would be to start by describing the magnetic field that surrounds each and every particle in the universe. The nature of matter dictates that these fields have vibrational qualities. This discovery was given the name "Quantum Activation" and was part of the body of work that earned Carlo Rubbia, the director of CERN, the world's largest particle physics laboratory, the Nobel Prize in 1984.

The particles of matter represent close to a billionth part of the natural energy field and, for this reason, are activated by the environment that these fields dominate. If we were to compare healthy tissue with that which has gone through pathological change, we would observe that, in the latter, there would be a much lower level of vibrational oscillation (the frequency increases when energy is being down-loaded and decreases when there is an energy drain); there is also, at the same time, a loss in the flexibility of that frequency.

In this situation compatibility with external impulses becomes more difficult (there is a loss of structure and balance) and incompatibility increases the gravity of the disorder. Long term change will eventually be accepted as normal by organisms and thus a level of natural compatibility is reached. Because of this, even chronic inflammation can become "dormant" because the body has become used to it.

To counter this, all the immune system requires is a small stimulation impulse. The effect of this is to give the immune system the appropriate data so as to stimulate a response. System Information Therapy's potency comes from using endogen (internal) frequencies and represents a cooperative effort with a healthy immune system. This is why, in patients with weak immune systems, the first stage of the therapy is an energy transfer (cell potential should be between 70 and 90 mV) to strengthen their system.

Clinical research has shown that even one session can be sufficient to register a change in the density of white corpuscles, a reverse in the decrease of lymphocytes (an indicator of weak immunity), and an increase to healthy and stable levels. All of this is possible after only a few weeks of treatment and a healthy immune system can be reinstated.

# Newtonian medicine's plumbers and the electro-technicians of vibrational medicine

When we study medical methodology we see that there are two distinctly separate approaches. The classic or conventional approach has been, as we have seen, dubbed the Newton model and within the existing healthcare systems this can be considered to be the most widespread. This approach could be summarized in the same way as Newtonian physics, but instead of the universe it is the human organism that is considered as a complex but mechanical system governed by laws. Orthodox physicians regard the body as biological machine controlled by the brain and nervous system.

In the Newtonian model, human physiological and psychological behavior is directed by a program within the brain and nervous system. For example, the heart is considered no more than a pump to provide the brain and body with oxygen from the blood's circulation. Doctors are so confident in their knowledge of that organ that they have developed an artificial mechanical pump that can actually take its place. The same developments have been made with hemodialysis, where a machine with a semi-porous membrane acting as an artificial kidney is used to remove toxic waste from the blood in the event of renal failure.

Thus,. while great strides have been made in bio-medical technology in replacing malfunctioning organs, the same cannot be said for our ability to use the Newtonian model to get to the root of disease and its causes and the ways to improve protection from it. In the Newtonian age it was a quite natural assumption for people to consider the body to be a biological machine, but unfortunately it is a belief that continues still up to this day in much of academic medicine. The pioneers of the Newtonian model were surgeons and their early surgical explorations tried to conceptualize the human body as a complex plumbing system. In our own time there have been many technical advances, but essentially the concept remains no more than the same: bio-plumbing. This is an almost unquestioned approach that centers on removing or repairing the ailing part of an organ or in some cases removing the organ altogether and replacing it with a healthy one, so that it functions again. Even with more recent advances in pharmacology, the approach remains intrinsically the same: repair and replace. Advances in molecular biology too, have been driven by the concept of effective repairs to this mechanical system with the minimum of side effects.

One would be foolhardy to deny all the benefits of many of these advances made in surgery and pharmacology and their importance in specific applications. However, when we consider life as a whole, and when we attempt to describe it only in terms of our cardio-vascular system, then it falls well short of a satisfactory explanation.

The components of a mechanical system are expressed as a whole; however, in our organism it is the energy created by the subtle (etheric) life-force that dictates the form and the molecular components that can be expressed as the whole. For this reason our body expresses itself with Gestalt consciousness rather than with our defining physical systems. The life-force is present in all living things, continually renewing the cells and creating order. When the life-force abandons the organism, the physical mechanism turns into an uncontrolled series of chemical reactions and functions and nothing more. This is the most important difference between the animate and the inanimate.

Unfortunately, orthodox medicine with its Newtonian approach most often chooses to ignore this. The reason for this is that there is still not a sufficient weight of academic scientific proof to explain or define what life-force energy is. This is the important variance between the occidental and oriental approach to medicine. The approach or belief of Western medicine is that this mechanical characterization of the human body makes it easier to perceive and manage. In ancient times the life-force and life-energy were considered extremely significant; the industrial revolution and the ensuing mechanical theoretic developments helped, however, to support the Newtonian view. With the fall of one apple, Newton's work on gravity and acceleration and the contributions his findings made to science opened the way for many new discoveries.

Nevertheless, whatever the contributions to the understanding of gravity and movement of objects might have been, there was, with the passing of time, next to no attempt to understand—let alone explain—electrical and magnetic fields. It was only when Newtonian physics became inadequate in explaining the creation of the universe and the form the universe took that researchers started to investigate these fields with more diligence. In more recent times, a handful of medical researchers have had the courage to begin research into life-force energy as the source of life; however, their approach has been still very much rooted in the bio-mechanical tradition. Physiological models have been approached from a solid matter vantage point and, unfortunately, the development of cells in bio-energy fields has been ignored almost entirely.

With the development of quantum physics the concept of matter has taken on a new understanding, with matter and energy having the ability to transpose one and other while at the same time existing in their own right. In contrast to the understanding of classical physics, the concepts of timelessness and placelessness were being promoted and the idea that two things could be found at the same time and at the same place (duality) began adding a new dimension. This developed from the concept that matter had two kinds of characteristics: particle and wave.

The approach that came to be known as the Einstein model was now slowly finding its place in the medical field. The Einstein approach to medicine is concerned with the energy of matter. The physicians who practice this are not just concerned with discovering the reasons for disease, but rather their energies are also directed at devising the most enduring forms of healing and treatment. Research is directed at the high energy etheric body that supplies our physical body. The holistic approach evolved from this, meaning that emotions, psyche and the metaphysical should be embraced as a whole in matters of health. The physical body began to be redefined as a complex network of life-energy that gave animation to the form. This subtle energy system was, in fact, what controlled the body's electro-physiological and hormonal functions at the cellular level.

As opposed to the symptom-based reduction approach of Newtonian medicine, the new approach was to consider and treat the multi-faceted nature of disease itself. Focus was directed at the importance of our energy body during the healing process so that a number of new, exciting energy-based diagnosis and treatment options, supportive and free of side effects, have been developed. Viewed in this light, the characterizations of Newtonian medicine as a plumber and Einsteinian medicine as an electro-technician are eminently apt.

# VI

# The Impotance of Resonance Energy to Our Physical and Subtle Bodies

Some readers would be forgiven for asking what the Secret's Secret has to do with our bodies. The reason, as it happens, is singularly clear. The potent energy force of our bodies is what brings the resonance phenomenon into place. Without this force resonance is almost inconceivable. This is why the holistic health of our bodies is vital to our resonance potential. What is called the aura is no more than the energy field that envelopes the body three dimensionally. It is created from the energetic body and its dimensions are directly related to the health of the physical body. Generally speaking, people who are full of affection and have a positive outlook will have a wide aura and possess high resonance energy.

Similarly, those who have a strong aura have a strong resistance to effects by external influences; those with weak auras are frequently more susceptible to the negative effects of external influences. The energy field that makes up the aura creates our "subtle bodies." The subtle body is formed in layers of differing densities around our physical body. The most important function of the subtle body is to organize and coordinate the emotional, psychological and spiritual responses.

Whatever amount of energy the mitochondria organelles might produce during the physical body's metabolism, the main supply of the body's energy is obtained from the subtle energy body. Our aura energy fields generate part of their energy requirements within the field and another part they obtain from cosmic energy which, put in simple terms, they convert into body electricity.

All individuals have their own independent energy supplies. This system differs from individual to individual depending on external factors and transmission. This is because each individual's aura has a unique vibrational frequency and this is where the secret of vibrational medicine is concealed.

While examining how the aura is part of the subtle body, we will study the significance of the vibrational frequencies of our bodies and how the information's code system is transmitted to our physical bodies. We will see what an extraordinary piece of quantum technology our bodies are, with the vibrational frequencies drawing comparisons with an electromagnetic telegraph system.

In the 1940s the Yale neuro-anatomist, Harold S. Burr, initiated work investigating the energy fields around living plants and animals. Burr delineated the dimensions of these electromagnetic fields and demonstrated that every growing organism has a template and that this is organized by the electromagnetic field. Burr's discoveries were backed up when electrographic photography techniques were developed that would show the holographic construction of the bio-energy fields.

Electrographic photography also goes under the name of Kirlian photography, a term we have referred to earlier. This kind of photography constitutes a way of recording images of animate objects by placing them in a high-frequency, high-voltage but low-amperage electrical field, a work pioneered in the 1940's by Russian researcher Semyon Kirlian.

An image produced by combining Kirlian electro-photographic techniques with Burr's electrical calculations resembles the sun's corona when photographed at total eclipse. This has been given the name Kirlian Aura. Using Burr and

Kirlian's discoveries, major changes in the electromagnetic fields of patients suffering from serious illness such as cancer have been observed. These findings have been corroborated when measured in controlled conditions and give a strong indication of the future direction of medicine. In another study, and by using the same photographic techniques, the toes of patients were photographed revealing important indications to serious future conditions such as cancer and cystic fibrosis.

In another fascinating study, Kirlian photographs were taken of a series of plant leaves in their complete form and then later, with a part, up to a third, missing. The surprising revelation was that in the photographs of the incomplete leaves they appeared to be whole. This has been called the Phantom Leaf Effect and is seen as an important proof of the existence of the bio-energy template.

The three dimensionality and organizational effects of biological energy fields have also been shown to have holographic properties. The Romanian researcher Dr. Ion Dumitrescu used electrographic techniques to photograph a leaf with the central part removed. The result was a secondary image within the removed part of a leaf also with a hole in its center. These studies are extremely important in supporting the concept of a body-enveloping energy field and the holographic characteristics of the etheric body. Just like the hologram, the etheric body is an energy form created from initial waves.

Who can tell, perhaps even the vast expanse of the universe is nothing more than a cosmic hologram. This is not such a fantastic notion either, as quantum and laser physicists Russel Targ and Harold Puthoff working at the Stanford Research Center in 100 Paulo Alto, California, proposed, as a result of their research, just such a cosmic hologram. Their projection was of a many layered hologram encompassing the universe's different dimensions so that we could think of the whole as one extraordinary single hologram made up of the accumulated data. When astronomers have concentrated on one point in space using different equipment and observational methods, they have come up with startlingly different results changing completely long held views about the structure of the cosmos.

The physical body is contiguous with vibrational energy with the suggestion that there are four further bodies. These are, in sequence, the etheric body, the emotional body, the mental body and the spiritual body. These bodies all lie within the aura with a far more complex transition than this simple description suggests, but for now, with the reason of locating healthy vibrational modes, we can refer to them in this way.

Although our energy body envelopes our body in layers, at the same time it is also absorbed at a low level into the rest of our body. We may think of this in the same way as radio or television waves. In actual fact, it is as though we are swimming in these wave signals. However, because of our physical limitations we are unable to feel these vibrational waves, just as we cannot hear sound in a frequency range above or below the capability of our hearing.

Our energy bodies are just one part of the whole cosmic vibration and what gives them their unique characteristics are their vibrational frequencies. An image of the human body has been created using Kirlian photographic technology. Now that there appears to be insurmountable evidence that these bodies exist, it would be wise to consider them one by one in the light of this understanding.

## The Human Energy Bodies and Aura

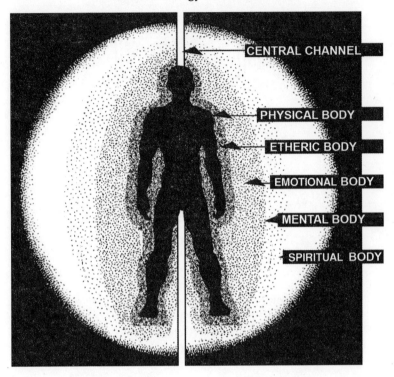

CENTRAL CHANNEL

PHYSICAL BODY

ETHERIC BODY

EMOTIONAL BODY

MENTAL BODY

SPIRITUAL BODY

## Phantom Leaf Phenomenon

# Creating a Hologram

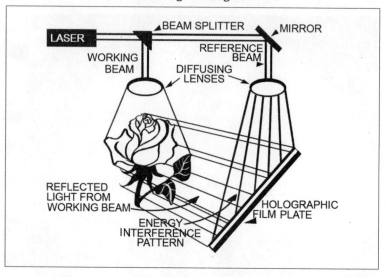

## The Holographic Structure of Living Things
The principal of Holography: Every component has the information of the whole within it.

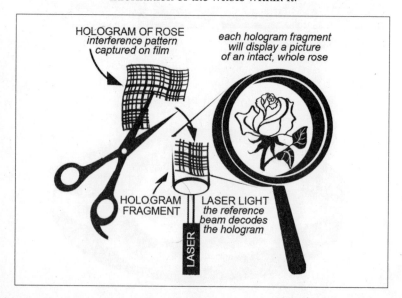

# The Physical Body

Unlike the subtle body, the physical body is the one that we can feel and see with our eyes. The reason the physical body is the densest of the bodies is that its energy or vibration frequency is much lower than the others. The physical body has an energy field with a dynamic vibrational frequency. It should be emphasized that although the physical body's vibrational energy field might be elevated, it is solid because it is in communication or coalesced with lower energy systems.

If we are to examine the physical body from a broad perspective we must begin to understand the nature of disease and healing and the significance of recovering good health with a far clearer perception. Would we ever have imagined that despite there being an almost imperceptible level of vibrational energy around us and without many of us ever feeling it, there is more knowledge than ever about vibrational medicine available?

We can see that the entity which we have habitually thought of as "matter"(including our physical body) is in fact worthy of far greater consideration when we think of how the atoms are made up of even smaller particles and that the atoms form molecules that in turn make up the cells and so the progression goes on, shaped and formed, as it is, by vibrational energy templates. In other words, it is just as Einstein defined in his description of quantum philosophy, "Matter equals energy, energy equals matter;" in other words, matter can be turned into energy and energy into matter.

The physical body is continually in an interchange with the vibrational fields that surround it, or with transmissions on electromagnetic frequencies. As a result of this interchange the physical body is, in one way or another, always surrounded by the energy of a different vibrational field. Thus, from time to time, the frequency of our bodily vibration will form a sympathetic vibration with one or other of these energy fields, or, in other words, the frequencies will be in harmony and bring with it whatever properties it possesses, but always with an outcome for our physical bodies. Perhaps this can be best explained with this example: Let us imagine a room in which there are two violins and that the strings of one of the violins have all been tuned to middle "c." When the violinist picks up the other violin in the opposite corner of the room and plays the same note we would hear the strings of the other violin resonating in harmony.

This example is important as it explains how one energy field can subtly affect another. As a result, human health is closely related to these energy fields that we are literally swimming in, which can impact us both positively and negatively. We must understand how certain energy healing techniques are vital for our physical body's health and how we can implement them. Vibrational medicine demonstrates its prominence most vigorously in this domain.

## Etheric Body

Following the publishing of the evidence presented using Kirlian photography, the subsequent comments and research reinforced convictions about the etheric body and concluded that it is the first energy body joined to the physical body and plays a pivotal role in the flow of resonance energy. Although the etheric body merges with the physical body, it is possible to observe it as a presence beyond the bounds of the physical body.

The role of the etheric body is to provide the energy templates for the physical body's maintenance and healing, almost like an energy relay station. With the assistance of these templates or matrices, the body's energy blockages are regulated and controlled at the etheric body level. The etheric body is harmonized with the vibrational frequencies of the organs, the circulatory system and the skeleton. The etheric body carries a three-dimensional blueprint of the organism's cells, tissue, organs and, indeed, of the whole life system itself.

Research has shown that the physical body's vitality is totally linked to the etheric body. The etheric body's existence does not come about as a result of the physical body but is present from birth. It is an inescapable fact that, just as disorders of the physical body affect the etheric, disorders of the etheric affect the physical.

There is a point that should not be overlooked: the etheric body is not just affected by the physical body, it can similarly be affected by all of the other subtle energy bodies. Like it or not, just as vibrational disorders in the etheric body manifest themselves as symptoms of "illness" in the physical body, these developments also find their negative response in the emotional, mental and spiritual bodies.

As Michael Talbot so succinctly put it in his book *Holographic Universe*, any disorder diagnosed in the etheric body will, weeks or even months later, eventually emerge in the physical body.

Dr. Richard Gerber expresses the idea that the etheric body has the function of something like a holographic energy template in guiding and directing the healthy development of the physical body. In short, the etheric body is nothing less than an energy matrix that has the function of forming and multiplying all the cells of the physical body. Furthermore any frequency disorders within the etheric body will, in time, appear in a similar form in the physical body.

We should never forget that every individual is like a ball of energy and that each individual's organ and metabolic system frequencies are always totally unique. So, while conventional medicine concentrates solely on a disorder's symptoms, we should consistently be concentrating on the causes. There is little benefit to our long term health in methods that remain within the diagnosis and treatment approaches.

The most striking characteristic of the physical body and its connected subtle bodies is how vital to human health the etheric body is, and the role it plays, along with the frequency differences that are the basis of vibrational medicine.

# Emotional Body

After the etheric body comes the emotional body. Some examples of its function can be expressed thusly: The emotional body is that entity that makes up our personal characteristics and carries the vibrations of our emotional make-up. It defines what we feel about ourselves and what level of engagement we have with the outside world. The emotional body closely resembles those of the physical and etheric bodies and generally has a fluid shapeless form. If we were to visualize senses as the colors of the spectrum, it is considered that our emotions would be like energy stains. These stains in affirmative and very sensitive individuals are light colored and shining, while they are dark colored in individuals with confused emotions.

The emotional body has a higher level of energy than the etheric body. It contains our senses and is also the depository for our conscious and unconscious data. As the emotional body is concerned with the energy of our emotions, it can, with the aid of energy channels connecting the bodies, influence the physical body both affirmatively and negatively—the latter taking the form of emotional imbalance, disorders to the brain's neuro-chemical activities and disorders to the body's energy processing.

Our emotional expression of our senses affects our physical body at the hormonal level and consequently at the cellular level having, respectively, a positive or negative influence.

The cornerstone for the synthesis of a healthy life is "love" and the vital source of this is found in the emotional body. This body is also the energy level depository for physical desire, appetite and yearning, the spiritual condition, senses and fears.

Therein lies the miraculous solution to protect us from the emotional storms of our interior worlds: Love! Love begins with loving ourselves first. Those who cannot love themselves can never know the real meaning of love. Those who do not love themselves also have a very low energy level in their emotional bodies. The greatest number of disorders in this body emerge from such causes as fear, fatalism, self-deprecation, anger, self-pity and guilt. Those who love themselves and fill their interior world with affection have—instead of negative emotions—contentment, tenderness and affirmative thoughts.

The emotional body is the source of the etheric body's consciousness and this is why the effects of resonance energy are so paramount; at the same time, in order to maintain the life-force, the emotional body is also connected to the etheric body.

In essence, all the body's experiences are interconnected, which is why they must possess a healthy vibrational frequency so that they can maintain a balanced and harmonized vibrational frequency with the other bodies. It is an inescapable fact that if one of the bodies is unhealthy it impacts negatively on all the other bodies. Similarly, the starting point for a healthy life is for the five bodies to function in balanced harmony.

## Mental Body

The mental body is processor and depository of all our thoughts, beliefs and intelligence. The mental body is one energy field level above the emotional body. The mental body is characterized by a yellow colored light that is perforated with small light points of different shape and density signifying the form and manner in which the person is thinking. The mental body is connected by the subtle energy channels to the lower bodies. The transmission through these channels to the physical body directly affects the endocrine and nervous systems. These effects on mental matrices in healthy individuals are affirmative, while in individuals who are scatter-brained and inattentive the effect is quite the opposite.

If our mental body is healthy, our thinking becomes clearer with our mental energy more focused, stronger and more effective; our purpose becomes clear and the power to fire up resonance energy becomes ever more apparent. Because our thoughts are formed in mental energy matrices that, in time, take shape both in the conscious and the subconscious, they thus reinforcing character and identity within the mental body. People with strong mental and intelligence skills have a positive influence on the emotional, the etheric and the physical bodies, which are all then observed to be functioning in balanced harmony. The basic reason for high mental capacity and intelligence is simply that of "equilibrium," for the way for us to keep our mental body productive is through balance. This is why various damaging addictions, because they directly affect psychological balance and function, are so detrimental to our total health. The simple explanation for morbid thought is a mental body bereft of equilibrium.

The first steps we can take to ensure equilibrium are to construct affirmative, attractive mental models and then turn them into words.

If there is a golden key for opening the locked doors of affection and emotion, then that key is equilibrium, which brings the mind's hidden canyons into the light of day. The health of our mental body is summed up in these two concepts: love and equilibrium. And what we must do is to confront every negative event with love and equilibrium and elevate our health to higher levels by overcoming stress. We should never forget that, just like the Sufi approach, "The mind is like a parachute, it only functions when it is opened."

## Spiritual Body

The spiritual body is a reflection of our Gestalt consciousness and is not only a higher body joined to the mental body but it is also combined with it. Compared to the other bodies it has the highest energy level and is the body that affects the power of the resonance energy frequency. The dictionary definition describes Gestalt consciousness as the approach whereby all mental activity is considered as a whole within the organism.

If any situation is fragmented and then pieced together it would be easy to miss what the real meaning or purpose of that situation. In other words, the sum of the parts are greater than the whole. And this sums up the spiritual body; it is what makes the human, human and can be considered the greatest of the four bodies. As a result of this, the spiritual body expresses the lived experiences of our Gestalt consciousness.

This consciousness, rather than being made up of concrete thought, is formed from abstract thought and concepts, that is to say, it is not based on the details of the subject but rather the underlying concepts and the subject as a whole. Thus to maintain a healthy spiritual body, we must try to conceptualize the mental process as a whole, as opposed to the unhealthy spiritual body that fails to conceptualize the whole but struggles to reach comprehension from the fragments. The result of this is that if we become stuck on the components we will never be able to comprehend the reality of the whole.

The most important aspect of the spiritual energy level is not the form or concept that emotions, ideas and thoughts take but the significance of the whole. Unlike the other bodies, including the physical body, the spiritual body goes beyond, surpassing all individual egos. As it is connected to all the universes, and in spite of a strong magnetic effect, its physical body energy and electrical effects are amply concentrated.

The significance of the spiritual body's magnetic energy is that it has the power to heal. Because the disorders and imbalances in this energy body can also permeate through the lower bodies, the end result can only be illness and bad health at the physical level. Similarly this body's power to heal permeates down through the lower bodies. Put another way, it can be described as an information and energy current that flows from the spiritual body to the mental body and from there to the emotional body, through the etheric body and eventually to find its end in the physical body.

One may conjecture that the spiritual body is to be found at a higher level than the other bodies; however, as the purpose of this book is to look at the more concrete research and studies of the subject, let us not diverge from that path here, but should you wish to read further of the more esoteric you can find a number of sources to help you.

# VII

## What We Must Do For the Health of Our Bodies

When we mention health, the first thing that comes to mind is orthodox medicine. This is because we have been taught to think of ourselves merely as a bio-physical organism. In the previous chapter we discussed the approach of Newtonian medicine and emphasized how the human organism is far more advanced than a chemical reaction driven machine. We further emphasized that the human body should not be regarded as just a cellular system and attempted to explain that there was little to be gained by approaching our health from a bio-plumbing point of view.

Following that, we started to examine the importance of vibrational medicine as a branch of quantum medicine. We concluded by observing that if we were to combine conventional medicine's approach with that of vibrational medicine we would have the true holistic approach to human health. In other words, vibrational medicine needs to be seen as complementary and in a supportive role to conventional medicine. We also discussed how holistic health cannot begin and end with just the physical body and that the other four bodies must be included in healthcare. Now we will look at what we can do to maintain the health of all five bodies.

While doing so we must pay attention to the following general health rules that can be applied to the physical and, by association, to the other four bodies:

Necessary rules for maintaining physical body health

- Consume a balanced and healthy diet.
- Get sufficient physical activity.
- Drink sufficient water and liquids.
- Only use anti-acids, antidepressants, antibiotics and anti-inflammatories when needed and never for extended periods of time.
- Protect ourselves against air and other pollution.
- Stay clear of cigarettes, alcohol and other addictive substances.
- Take great care to have a healthy digestive and bowel system.
- Get enough sleep.

What must be done for the other four bodies can be summarized thusly: The most significant threat to the health of the etheric, emotional, mental and spiritual bodies comes from stress. The major causes of stress are a permanent negative attitude, an inability to control fears and being isolated from affection and success. It is important to remember that any disorder that threatens one of the bodies also has an effect on the others.

## Physical bodily health

Our physical energy body and our material body work in holistic partnership. As we mentioned in the previous chapter, just as energy can be transformed into matter, so can matter be transformed into energy. The most important rule for general well-being is a healthy metabolism. The physical body sustains life through the process of cellular metabolism.

When the holistic partnership goes astray, the body can begin to experience problems. The risk of metabolism disorders leading to cancer is extremely high, for instance.

The mitochondria organelles are the units in cells that produce energy, almost like small power stations, while at the same time they maintain the cell's respiration. The power unit of the mitochondria is a chemical molecule called ATP (andenosine triphosphate). The organelle coverts the potential energy of food molecules into ATP. The healthiness of the metabolic energy produced by the ATP entirely depends on the healthiness of our diet. That is why the importance of the quality of what we consume as food and drink cannot be emphasized enough.

Generally speaking, metabolism can be described as the process whereby the nutritive components of food (matter) are converted into energy by the mitochondria, after which they are converted into bio-chemical (matter) components, as and when required, to meet the body's needs. In short, just as we have noted before, matter is turned into energy and energy into matter and, as long as we are alive, this process continues.

Bioenergetics is the study that conjoins conventional or orthodox medicine with complementary or alternative medicine. The Newtonian school of medicine supports the traditional approach whereas the Einstein school proposes the use of vibrational medicine. Apart from their different academic approaches we have frequently made the analogy of bio-plumbing and bio-electro technology. Thus conventional medicine focuses on the material body while complementary medicine places the focus on energy.

The main theme of this book has been to concentrate on the resonance phenomenon, energy, self-esteem and love, while at the same time—so as not to lose continuity—approaching these from an energy perspective. This is purposeful, as the most significantly unifying aspect is that of holistic well-being.

That is to say well-being is a concept that encapsulates the physical material body as well as those of the upper or subtle energy bodies so that it must be regarded and cared for as a whole.

The interest in health matters has never been stronger, with television, the Internet and the written media inundating us with information on how to lead a healthy life. Although not all the information is always helpful, we can see that the population is gradually becoming more knowledgeable about their own health. Thus we need not go into minute detail here regarding care for the health of our physical body.

However, there are three subjects that are not widely understood and that I believe to be vital to the health of everyone. I am compelled to include them here:

The first of these is the subject of probiotics and the digestive tract. The second is comprehensive detoxification, by which we do not mean superficial methods such as a liquid diet course, vitamin or mineral supplements, or colon cleansing; what we will examine here is the deep comprehensive detoxification of toxin build-up in the connective tissue. The third subject is the pH levels of our bodies or, the acid-alkali balance of our organisms. The significance of this is that for an efficient metabolism, maintaining the correct pH balance is of paramount importance. The majority of what we usually eat is acidic. A chronically acidic body medium means corroded body cells. Just as acid eats away at surfaces, it eats away at our bodies. The medical term for this is acidic hemorrhaging. Despite this, few individuals ever consider taking a regular blood test to control their pH levels. But this is something that we should address as seriously as the adequate consumption of probiotics and comprehensive detoxification.

## Probiotics

The physical body has one system of organs that is crucial to our existence and yet most of us would place it far down on our list of vital organs. In complementary medicine this vital system of organs is the "second central nervous system." Of course, we are referring to the digestive tract. There is a constant chemical and electrical interaction between it, the central nervous system and the brain. Scientists have a simple expression for this: the "brain-gut" current. Research has reinforced the importance of the entire tract and the lower gastrointestinal tract in particular, dubbed the "second brain." When viewed superficially, it would appear to come second to the respiratory system.

As we acknowledge that the surface area of the gastrointestinal tract is approximately 300 square meters or almost the entire surface area of a tennis court, we must also understand that the "second brain" most certainly should not be ignored. The consumption of fried food, processed food with dyes, additives, artificial sweeteners, sugar or flour, along with alcoholic beverages, all represent challenges thrown down to the "second brain." Not only can all of these cause chronic constipation, with time such consumption leads to failure of the health of the central nervous system and a lowering of the shield of the immune system.

The highest risk is colon cancer. Left untreated, this cancers can soon spread with its quatro-polar relationship to the other organs (lungs, liver, kidneys). The easiest way to avoid this bleak outcome is to be careful what we eat and drink. In the course of a lifetime we send nearly 60 tons down our digestive tract. We must recognize the daily danger that our bodies face from a list of risks found in what we eat and drink: viruses, harmful bacteria, fungi, yeasts, harmful chemicals and heavy metals to name but a few.

For this reason probiotics, prebiotics and synbiotics should be essential components of our diets. Probiotics, which means "for life," are friendly and beneficial microorganisms or bacteria that maintain the delicate balance between beneficial flora and harmful bacteria and aid the processes of the gastrointestinal tract.

**Some foods with a probiotic content**

- Yogurt
- Chicory
- Kefir
- Asparagus
- Soft Cheese
- Ginger
- Olives
- Fresh soya bean sprouts

- Garlic
- Ayran
- Red pepper
- Pineapple
- Pickled cabbage
- Hazelnuts, walnuts and hard shell nuts.

## Prebiotics

Briefly, prebiotics provide the nutritional environment for probiotics to flourish.

**Some examples of prebiotic foods that provide a nutritional environment for healthy probiotic activity**

Artichoke
Beans
Spinach
Chickpeas
Chard
Lentils
Red/black cabbage
Flax
Red/black chicory
Goat's milk
Tomatoes

Strawberries and various blackberries
Onion
Banana
Barley
Whole wheat (not flour)
Oats
Mustard leaves
Pulses
Miso soup

## Synbiotics

Synbiotics are foods and supplements that combine the properties of prebiotics and probiotics. Yogurt and kefir grains are good examples of these and daily consumption of an appropriate amount of each is recommended.

Because they are in tandem, our physical energy body cannot be separated from our physical material body. The same can be said for what has been termed our "second brain." Most crucial is that we abandon the notion that we are mechanisms run by a few chemical reactions and accept that we are a far more advanced and complex organism. I repeat: it is erroneous to regard the human organism as just a cellular system.

Treatment by pharmaceutical products is a complex intervention of a biomechanism that includes the body's organs, enzymes and receptors. Successful applications can remove or limit the illness's symptoms and bring a measure of relief to the patient. Even though it is essential that an investigation into the causes and origins of the disorder are also carried out, many doctors overlook this, preferring to regard the human organism as a complex piece of machinery. Of course, this is not true of all doctors and I am not trying to belittle the contribution of conventional medicine. Nonetheless, there has never been such a need as there is today for sophisticated doctors who understand and can examine the biological mechanism at the molecular vibrational level.

## Real Detoxification

Our body is such a phenomenal system that it is capable of a completely miraculous renewal and elimination of all toxic substances from the system. A truly healthy body has the capacity to overcome all illnesses unaided. Of course, the first question that comes to our minds is, "Why then do we become ill?"

The reason is simple: we overload our bodies with an unsupportable level of toxins. The body is unable to cope with this kind of level of toxins and illness quickly follows. This is why the importance of detoxification is so paramount. For most people "detoxification" conjures an image of freshly squeezed fruit juice diets, soup diets, the use of various vitamin and amino acid supplements or even colon cleansing.

True detoxification is far more profound and essential. According to the latest medical information, mesenchyme or ground substance matrix, a component of soft connective tissue, plays an important role in today's typical degenerative illnesses. Matrix is a form of fibrous tissue made up of elastin, collagen and glucosamine and is interconnected to the cells of the organs of the circulatory, nervous and lymphatic systems where it forms the infrastructure for providing nutrition to the organs' cellular systems. Outside factors such as excessive acid, food additives, industrial chemicals, genetically destroyed foodstuffs, excessive alcohol use, tobacco products, caffeine, substance addictions, chronic inflammation and infections, environmental pollution, poor and incorrect nutrition, physical and mental stress and a generally unhealthy lifestyles can seriously threaten this matrix and aversely affect the cellular nutrition of the organs.

The end results are chronic illness, allergies, weak immune systems, chronic skin disorders, depression and a myriad of other conditions from aches and pain through to chronic disease. The unifying factor in these disorders is that they are highly resistant to treatment.

A reduction in the functionality of the matrix correspondingly reduces the nutrition and cleansing of the cells, which in time manifests as illness. Medication or other approaches of conventional methods fail to reach the organs' atrophied cells, so, in order to successfully treat specific illnesses, the matrix must first be cleansed of its "old loads" so as to give it the capability to repair itself.

The foremost complementary treatments directed specifically at the matrix are regeneration therapy, ozone therapy,

colon hydrotherapy, phytotherapy and homeopathic remedies. The cardinal rule in resorting to any of these methods is
that you are first under a physician's control and that you
drink plenty of water (as a rough guide, 40cc for every kilo of
weight). It is vital we drink enough water; just as gold prospectors use running water to flush out the gold, we must use plenty of water to flush out toxins and ensure that our bodies can
utilize nutrition in the best possible way. If we fail to take care
of our body it will certainly fail us. Just feeling "out of sorts,"
is sufficient reason to visit the doctor.

## The pH value (acid-alkali level) of our bodies

The fabric of a body subjected to chronic acidity will not only
corrode, it will begin to decompose as well. The total length of
the body's cardiovascular system, from arteries down to the
smallest blood vessel, is close to 97,000 kilometers long and the
number of cells is in the region of 75 trillion. Healthy cells form
healthy organs and healthy organs form healthy cells. For
example, the health of the endocrine and immune systems are
the foundation on which the whole body's health is built. An
exceptionally high acid level in our bodies immediately affects
our quality of life and is an open invitation for every type of
disease and premature ageing. The damage is first seen in the
arteries of the circulatory system, just as acid dissolves marble,
the body's acid begins to corrode the arteries.

pH value is, in essence, a measurement of hydrogen levels
for the pH value in the body affects the speed and effectiveness
of all the bio-chemical reactions. pH is measured on a scale of
1 to 14. The number 1 on the pH scale represents concentrated
acid, while 7 is distilled water and neutral. A healthy bodily
pH value is essential for a balanced blood circulation and for
the body's chemical order. If we consider that there are more
than 75 trillion cells and 97,000 kilometers of blood vessels in
the body, then their corrosion and decomposition will be
spread over a considerable period of time.

For example, let us consider the banana, found throughout the year in supermarkets. Bananas decompose from the inside outwards. We have all seen how the banana's skin changes in color from green to yellow and then to brown and finally, black. Just as most people will look in the mirror and declare themselves to be in good health, they are unaware that the problem lies within; that they are corroding and decomposing from the inside outwards. Fortunately, this is not true for everyone, but still perhaps the greater majority will start the day with a coffee (acid), following with a hamburger (acid) for lunch, washed down with a large carbonated drink (acid), and then the evening with perhaps an alcoholic drink before dinner, pasta perhaps, and all the while completely oblivious to the fact that their cells are corroding, organs decomposing and the whole body prematurely aging.

The body's bio-electrical system, inter cellular activity, enzymes and the processing of vitamins and minerals are perpetually affected by what we eat and the pH level of our blood. We must pay close attention to everything we eat, with particular emphasis on the digestive tract and the body's pH level. This is why, in addition to the list of probiotic and prebiotic foods given above, we will also include a list of acid, alkali and neutral foods below. It is not too difficult to memorize this list so that when we sit down to eat we can work out the pH balance of our diets, without forgetting about the importance of quantity and variety. To maintain a healthy pH level of approximately 7.4 we must have a diet rich in vitamins and minerals; therefore we must eat with as much variety as permitted. Thus what we eat becomes the best guarantee for a healthy life.

We can say "stop" to many disorders and put aging on hold by ensuring the correct pH level for a healthy gastrointestinal tract and for healthy cell regulation (a high circulatory hydrogen level) along with a healthy cell metabolism. Controlling our pH levels is quite easy and should be done frequently. Most pharmacies sell testing kits for either the urine or the saliva. But perhaps the best course is to can find a physician who is knowledgeable about the subject and have him/her test and advise you. Make sure you ask your physician about the importance of probiotics, prebiotics, detoxification and the pH levels of our blood. The purpose of this is to make sure that your doctor is abreast of the developments in modern medicine because it is a surprisingly small few physicians who are actually following developments and are knowledgeable on the subject or take it seriously enough to advise their patients correctly.

### Alkaline and acidic food lists

The figures in the right column of this list indicate the alkaline value of the food in question and how it affects our bodies. For example, if we compare raw spinach (+556) with grapefruit (+25) we can see that it is 20 times more efficacious. Similarly for the minus figures in the acidic food list.

# Alkaline Food list

| Food | Quantity | Effect | Food | Quantity | Effect |
|---|---|---|---|---|---|
| Raw Spinach | 4 cups | + 556 | Avocado | 1/2 cup | + 44 |
| Beet Greens | 1 cup | + 478 | Raisins | 1/2 cup | + 44 |
| Molasses | 1 tablespoon | + 360 | Dried Dates | 7 | + 40 |
| Celery | 5 stalks | + 341 | Green Beans | 1 cup | + 39 |
| Dried Figs | 5 | + 297 | Muskmelon | 1/4 | + 38 |
| Carrots | 3 | + 282 | Limes | 1/2 cup | + 33 |
| Dried Beans | 1/2 cup | + 282 | Sour Cherries | 18 | + 30 |
| Chard Leaves | 1 1/2 cups | + 214 | Tangerines | 2 | + 29 |
| Water Cress | 2 1/2 cups | + 192 | Strawberries | 12 | + 28 |
| Sauerkraut | 2/3 cup | + 176 | White Potato | 1 | + 26 |
| Leaf Lettuce | 1/2 head | + 170 | Sweet Potato | 1 | + 26 |
| Green Lima Beans | 2/3 cup | + 142 | Grapefruit | 1/2 cup | + 25 |
| Dried Lima Beans | 2/3 cup | + 123 | Apricot | 2 | + 25 |
| Rhubarb | 1 cup | + 117 | Lemon | 1/2 cup | + 24 |
| Cabbage | 1 1/3 cups | + 111 | Blackberries | 1 cup | + 22 |
| Broccoli | 1 cup | +101 | Orange | 1/2 cup | + 22 |
| Beets | 2/3 cup | + 98 | Tomato | 1 | + 21 |
| Brussels Sprouts | 6 | + 95 | Peach | 1 large | + 21 |
| Green Soy Beans | 2/3 cup | + 85 | Raspberries | 1 cup | + 19 |
| Cucumber | 10 slices | + 71 | Banana | 1 small | + 18 |
| Parsnip | 1/2 large | + 67 | Onion | 1 small | + 14 |
| Radishes | 7 | + 64 | Grapes | 1/2 cup | + 10 |
| Rutabagas | 3/4 cup | + 62 | Pear | 1 | + 10 |
| Dried Peas | 1/2 cup | + 57 | Blueberries | 2/3 cup | + 5 |
| Mushrooms | 7 | + 50 | Apple | 1 | + 5 |
| Cauliflower | 1 cup | + 50 | Watermelon | 1/2 slice | + 5 |
| Pineapple | 1 cup | + 44 | Green Peas | 3/4 cup | + 5 |

# Acidic Food list

| Food | Quantity | Effect | Food | Quantity | Effect |
|---|---|---|---|---|---|
| Scallops | 1/2 cup | - 226 | Whole Wheat Flour | 5/8 cup | - 26 |
| Oysters | 5 | - 209 | Salmon | 1 cup | - 26 |
| Dried Lentils | 1/2 cup | - 171 | Beef Steak | 1/4 pound | - 24 |
| Sausage | 6 links | - 160 | Turkey | 1/4 pound | - 23 |
| 127 Sardines | 8 | - 160 | Barley | 5/8 cup | - 21 |
| Oatmeal | 1 cup | - 95 | Veal Chops | 1 | - 21 |
| Corned Beef | 1/4 pound | - 80 | Lamb | 1/4 pound | - 17 |
| Lobster | 1/4 pound | -78 | White Bread | 2 slices | - 15 |
| Shrimp | 1/4 pound | - 78 | Wheat Bran | 1 tablespoon | - 10 |
| Haddock | 1/4 pound | - 78 | English Walnuts | 10 | - 10 |
| Soda Crackers | 8 | - 52 | Lamb Chop | 1 | - 10 |
| Codfish | 1/4 pound | - 51 | Bacon | 2 slices | - 10 |
| Pasta | 7/8 cup | - 50 | Eggs | 2 | - 9 |
| Peanut Butter | 3 tablespoons | - 49 | Whole Wheat Bread | 2 slices | - 8 |
| Chicken | 1/4 pound | - 43 | Pork Chop | 1 | - 6 |
| Peanuts | 57 | - 39 | Honey | 4 tablespoons | - 4 |
| Wheat Germ | 1 tablespoon | - 38 | Fresh Corn | 1/2 cup | - 2 |
| Brown Rice | 5/8 cup | - 29 | | | |

# Neutral pH foods list

| Food | Effect | Food | Effect |
|---|---|---|---|
| Milk (whole milk in particular) | 0 | Corn Oil | 0 |
| Butter (unsalted and natural) | 0 | Olive Oil | 0 |
| Corn Syrup | 0 | Most Vegetable Oils | 0 |
| Sugar | 0 | | |

Of course, these lists do not cover every food we might eat but as most of what we eat tends to be acidic we should try to stay away from too much of the following:

**Foods with the highest acidic value**

**Meat:** Beef, pork, veal, chicken, turkey, lamb, shell fish, canned tuna and sardines
**Dairy products:** Parmesan cheese and processed cheese.
**Nuts:** Peanuts, processed nuts.
**Beverages:** Alcoholic drinks, wine, beer, coffee, black tea.
**Sweeteners:** All artificial sweeteners.

We should also be aware of how we combine foods; imagine the damage you do to your body when too much alcohol is consumed, along with eating sausages or salami. As with everything, balance is the key to good nutrition. We must remember that everything we eat affects our body's pH level, just as everything we eat affects the metabolic function of our body. It would be prudent to keep these wise words from the father of medicine in mind:

"Let your food be your medicine and
let your medicine be your food."
Hippocrates

# The etheric body's health

There is an intersecting dimension to the etheric body and the physical body and, indeed, to the other bodies. The etheric body continually provides the physical body with vitality, life-force and endurance. It also helps to maintain equilibrium of our consciousness with the bioenergy principle. The etheric body is the physical body's subtle dimension. The etheric body has a higher level of electromagnetic energy than the physical body, while at the same time supporting sub-atomic particles.

This complex structure is connected to the physical body by meridian energy channels, or nadis.

The health of our etheric body is directly related to the way we think. The etheric body's most important energy source is the power of affirmative thought. Those with powerful affirmative thought processes have high energy reserves. A clear indication of the etheric body's health is whether our thought frequencies are high or low. As a result, the first symptoms of stress are disorders in the energy frequency of the etheric body. Energy disorders affect the physical body, and also have a detrimental effect on all the bodies of the aura, as the system of bodies is called.

The human being should be considered as consisting of a complex energy field and the physical-cellular body is part of a network connected to the other bodies of the system. Illness occurs when there are imbalances in this network. These imbalances form electrical blockages and the means to cure these is through the application of various methods and equipment found in vibrational medicine; however, the best method of overcoming imbalances caused by stress is simply to change our way of thinking.

Most of us are at a loss when it comes to how to overcome stress, but stress is an inescapable part of life. It is a vital element of being alive and in a continuous state of flux. It is our reactions to these changes that are the source of our stress. The Chinese believe that crisis should be regarded as an opportunity. By using methods that inspire, we should be able to succeed in thinking affirmatively. Many sources, and experience, have shown that there is no apparently irresolvable stress that cannot be overcome by thinking positively and being filled with love.

The secret of being healthy is to successfully resist and eliminate the assaults on the body caused by stress. The etheric body has a role as the bridge between the physical body and the other bodies of the aura. This is why, if our physical, emotional, mental and spiritual bodies are under stress, this stress is immediately transmitted to the etheric body. Stress is therefore most destructive on the etheric body, so it is vital to regulate any build-up of negative energy in this body. Being tense is a milder form of stress but it is actually quite natural and at times can be beneficial.

Relieving stress energy can require great effort, whereas relieving tension energy is much easier. It becomes possible to relieve the destructive effects of stress before it even happens. In some quarters, being tense is considered to be one secret of success. It has come to the point that the tension and nervousness of successful people is an indication of their power. The tenseness that makes us sensitive and interested in what is happening around us can only be positive. A life completely devoid of tension would be like soup without flavor. When we watch a football or basketball game we can be completely unaware of our own tension; it is only when we relax at the end of the game that we can feel the tension drain away and, only then, do we become aware it. These can be some of life's sweetest moments.

But let us consider for a moment those who cannot let go or who cannot relax. Stress is, inescapably, the outcome of unremitting tension. To summarize: The health of the etheric body is entirely dependent on how we manage our stress. The golden key for managing stress is to integrate affirmative thinking into our daily lives. If, despite all our good efforts, we are unable to relieve the energy blockages caused by stress, then there is another way for us to regain our health and that is by using biological resonance methods to clear the blockages in our energy channels. These methods will provide an uninterrupted life energy current, and with an immune system restored to health our bodies will be able to overcome any illness we encounter.

## The emotional body's health

If we desire to exit the stormy waters of fear, anger, hate and guilt and set sail on the warm calm waters of joy, tranquility and understanding, we must pay careful attention to the health of our emotional body. However settled "equilibrium" is in our mental body, "love's home is in our emotional body."

There is no barrier or hardship that cannot be overcome by those who possess equilibrium and are filled with love. These two golden words should never leave our thoughts; but the main cornerstone for a healthy and contented life is love.

We must apply the same level of care to exercising our emotional bodies as we do our physical bodies. We can begin by asking ourselves, on any given evening or at any time when we are resting or at peace with the world, "What can I do to fill the energy reserves of my emotional body?" We ask this question and wait for our emotions to come up with the answer and in doing that we have started to exercise our emotions.

There are different answers to that question and different methods, but it is best for each individual to determine what suits them. Before beginning anything though, the most critical thing we must do to prepare ourselves is to start loving ourselves. Quite simply, if we fail to do that, the failure of whichever emotional exercise we choose is almost guaranteed. The love we are referring to here is not a form of egotism; learning to love yourself is something requiring dedication and emotion that is fed not by what you take from others, but by what you give.

The issue is one of mutual benefit; the decisions we make are tempered by what we give in return. We must put the interests of others before our own. "Loving" begins with loving ourselves, with the reward of being able to love others. It is not enough to think, "Well, of course I love myself." The road to love is long. This is because our emotional body is capricious and to put our interior world in order requires dedication, patience and perseverance. However, once we have set our hearts to this course, success is assured. Try it and you will see.

We can take our first steps on this journey by standing in front of the mirror and looking deeply into the eyes that confront us. What do you see? With all your integrity, describe what you see. Is it someone who is at peace and loves him or herself or is it someone who is not pleased with his or her physical appearance or emotional, intellectual or spiritual self? Is it someone who is constantly blaming others but who acts guilty? Is this person burdened with problems, anger, fears and guilt? Which is the one you see?

If you see that there could be a problem, immediately begin to think in the affirmative and with an open heart, begin to define what it is. This is the first step to clarifying the issue, should one exist. With an affirmative outlook the first condition of any problem is that "if there is a problem, there must be a solution."

You can try these exercises when you set out on this essential path.

- Have confidence that you have enough intelligence, patience, and strength to resolve any problem.
- Concentrate calmly and intently thinking what the solutions to the problem might be.
- Make sure you know the fundamental that 'the seeds of success and freedom lie at the heart of every problem."
- Make sure that you analyze the problem's smallest details and step back and look at it from different angles.
- Generate different solutions and then compare them.
- Make a step by step plan of how much you are prepared to do and sacrifice on this journey.
- Until you have a solution that you can accept do not brood on it, but be formative and productive and always patient.
- Always remain empathetic.
- Focus on developing a giving attitude, not a taking one.
- Do not always resort to blame, first remove the guilt from yourself and always be forgiving, both of yourself and others.
- Be at peace with yourself and with others.
- Make others happy and be happy yourself and for this reason you will start to love yourself.

Each time we resolve an emotional issue, we become more experienced, more righteous, stronger and, most important of all, more healthy. And the result is that these become the first steps in loving ourselves and we feel the seeds of love that lie within all of us start to germinate. Disaffection is an infectious disease; affection is an infectious state of good health.

To reinforce the feeling of love that begins to emerge within us, we can try another method of affirmation. Take a small notebook and mark each page with the days of the week ahead of you; each day record what you considered the most important event for you on that particular day. At the bottom of each page, note if you have helped or supported anyone in any way, whether you have created happiness or made anyone smile, whether you have made any sacrifices on anyone else's behalf. You may find that this exercise prompts you to begin each day by saying, "I must do something for someone else today." You may also find that as time passes, you will not even look at the empty space on the bottom of the page for prompts. This method of engaging with those around you will become a way of life, so much so that on some days you may even feel unfulfilled if you have not done anything worthy or selfless.

The result: acting selflessly will cause you to give up old selfish ways. Over time, selflessness may almost become an obsession. And truly, you will let go of your old opinion of yourself and begin to love the real you. You will begin to feel more affection, more love. You will develop a more mature understanding of your family, your friends and even those you meet in daily life. You will feel yourself begin to fill up with joy and happiness. It is important that you determine and use your own method, because everyone occupies their own separate world. Or in the language of vibrational medicine, everyone has a different vibrational frequency. This does not mean that we cannot share our experiences; there is great comfort in being able to say: "I now know how to love myself more and I am now someone full of love."

Let us look at how our emotional health can affect our physical health. If we view it from the vibrational medicine perspective, then a healthy emotional state is vital and directly affects physiology through various bio-chemical and energy channels. Our emotions affect cerebral waves, neuro-chemical patterns and the organs and glands of the body, and they also have an overall beneficial effect.

We can all witness the extraordinary power carried by our emotions, whether expressed or not. Try to keep Masuru Emoto's book, *Love Thyself,* within reach. Emoto offers an astonishing collection of photographs of ice crystals where we see how our emotions and thoughts can uniquely affect even water. This book of photographs records how each uniquely individual crystal was formed in response to positive thought, emotions, prayers, music and even writing.

As our physical body is almost seventy percent composed of water, we can begin to understand the powerful effect that thoughts and emotions can have on our physical body. That is why the health of the emotional body is essential and why we must practice these exercises to learn to love ourselves. Make them a part of your life and may affection-filled emotions always be with you.

## The mental body's health

Just as the emotional body expresses our emotions and nurtures the seeds of love and affection, it is in our mental body that we express our concrete thoughts and where our intelligence and intellect are balanced and developed. Our mental body is the source of all our thoughts and beliefs. The golden key for the health of our mental body is "equilibrium."

The emotional and mental bodies intercommunicate and that is why, for the sake of the health of our mental body, we must conceptualize these two elements together. We examined the emotional body under the love concept and now we examine the concept of equilibrium. I would like to start by referring to my book, *Pencere* (*Window,* in English). The road to a productive mental world passes through equilibrium and, in fact, the most important human characteristic after "love" is "equilibrium. "And why does love come first?" You might well ask. The answer is that it is difficult to achieve balance without love, just as it is impossible to find equilibrium without the energy that love gives. A healthy mental body represents the balance between our internal and external worlds. The most basic element to maintaining personal contentment and happiness is equilibrium. Just as our emotional body needs love for nourishment, so too does our mental body crave balance. A healthy mental body is not alone at the extremes but it is the body that observes the extremes to conceptualize a life of equilibrium. Knowledge is found in balance, because "right," "beauty" and "good" are all facets of equilibrium.

The events of the external world can be observed from different windows, each providing a different individual vantage point. One of the most important components of happiness is intelligence. If you are sad, it indicates that you are not content with your life—and if you cannot change that perception, you are not using your intelligence productively. Productive use of intelligence requires exercise, just as you might do your morning physical exercise.

Let us imagine that you are someone who has neglected physical exercise for several years. One day you are required to complete a heavy exercise routine. It is highly unlikely that you would be able to complete the routine. However, if it was broken down into lighter units built up over several days, there is no doubt that you would eventually successfully complete it. In exactly that same way we can start mental exercise.

There is one condition to mention first: just as physical exercise can be most effective in clear open air, mental exercise should be done with your mind free of anxiety and care. We understand that this is not always easy. Sadness, disaffection, failure and world-weariness must be identified and discarded so we can concentrate on happiness and hope from our mental window. After we have patiently learned to do this we begin to reap the benefits of the exercises.

If something has made you unhappy, imagine sweeping it out of your mind and throwing it away. Imagine that your mind is a vacuum and proceed to fill it with things that will make you happy in the future. Direct these thoughts to beauty and health. Your dreams are your thoughts, and your thoughts—as we have seen— are quantum energy. Difficult as it may be to conceive, these thoughts are imbued with amazing power. Try to visualize those ice crystals of almost divine beauty captured on film by Masaru Emoto; all are miraculously shaped with the power of positive thought. Now you are ready to start your mental gymnastics.

Either find a corner of your home where you can be alone and undisturbed, or go outside with the intention of a long walk. It is important that you have solitude. Begin by showing yourself respect; look back and acknowledge your successes. Be proud of your development and progress—not just in material success but in intangible achievements as well. Consistently think about good, about positive events and, prior to anything, make sure you are fully topped up with love. However difficult they may seem, mental gymnastics are not just about eliminating anguish and trouble. Perhaps at the beginning you can only maintain this state for a few minutes. Eventually you will be able to make it last longer and longer.

This represents the first step in taking control of your own mind. Emptyin, your mind and remaining inactive requires will-power and for that, exercise is essential. Formulating plans to make our dreams come true is also part of the exercise program. While making these plans we ensure no other thoughts enter our heads. We must be dedicated. Mental gymnastics can be summarized simply as concentrating for as long as possible on the affirmative and the things that will make us happy. These exercises are not just limited to realizing our optimistic dreams, they can also include our less lofty goals.

If, while doing this exercise and focusing on one item, you find that your mind skips to something unplanned, it is most likely an indication that you still have more work to do in this exercise. A successful session could be first deciding on your area of focus and then, following that plan through without deviation. If we carry out the program successfully with patience and perseverance we will see that we can direct our thinking and we have become the captains of our own destiny. And it is contentment that will take us to the horizons of our dreams, with the wind of affection filling our sails and speeding our way.

It is not just dreaming that will take us to our destination; every thought and dream we have are part of a reality, and the primary principle is love because together they create the resonance from which all energy comes. This is the secret of the healthy mental body, to have a foundation of love and equilibrium with which to set out on the journey to success. We do this so that instead of losing our way with success, we are shaped with love. These words of Gautama Buddha should bring comfort and help us in remembering the true meaning of success with equilibrium when we meditate on it.

"Everything rises and falls on this shining path,
The moment we see this, we should find
ourselves above all sorrow."

To paraphrase, we should not forget that we live in a bi-polar world, and that every joy and every sorrow is transient. Each one of us is consumed by sorrow, fear, anxiety and phobias, all of which are humankind's most bitter foes. As all things do pass, we should not even consider negativity, and first and foremost we must attempt to embrace and love ourselves, becoming a person overflowing with love. This is the shinning path of the Buddha's words.

# The Spiritual body's health

In the previous chapter, while referring to the spiritual body, we discussed how it reflected the Gestalt consciousness and how Gestalt encapsulates the idea that the sum of the parts is greater than the whole. Gestalt therapy is a method used in psychiatry that ostensibly is directed at the spiritual body. The four other bodies form egg-shaped layers and at the crown chakra of the spiritual body is our "karma." The original Sanskrit meaning of "karma" is "act, action or performance." The allegorical definition of karma is that it is humankind's databank. Every thought, effect, event, action—everything we do—is recorded in this memory, just like the memory of your computer. The computer memory records in binary language, the karma similarly, but in terms of what is positive and what is negative. All the negative data, just like bad memories, come to the surface again and again and can seriously imperil our health.

The negative energy of unresolved karma is the source of much of our ill-health and sorrow. If we look back at events that have gone wrong in our lives, we will see that nine out of ten times they can be attributed to karma. There is only one solution and that is to resolve our karma. As long as our karma remains in an unresolved state, our Gestalt consciousness is threatened with any number of psychological disorders. Unresolved karma always returns. All the negative thoughts we transmit around us will come flying back at us like so many boomerangs.

I have referred to how the incorrect approach to an unhealthy spiritual body is to break problems into components, thus making it impossible to get anywhere near resolution. Instead, we must perceive karma as a whole. Just when everything appears to be going well, an unresolved karma event can re-emerge to cause turmoil. Karma uses energy to record every event of our lives and when these remain unresolved they manifest themselves as karmic disorders. Determining the reason behind these can then be difficult.

To balance the health of our spiritual body we must find a reason to concentrate and focus intently on something. Prayer and meditation are most effective in helping us to resolve the problem; there are also various exercises we can use. Perhaps as a last resort, we can seek psychological and psychiatric support. It is essential to be able to stand back and observe the events of our lives from a distance and see them as a whole; we should be able to comprehend that our negative thoughts will, in the course of time, create new issues for us to confront.

The negative events of our lives repeat themselves over and over, like a needle stuck in the groove of an old vinyl record. If, instead of constant repetition, we were to see the whole, including the negative events, we would be able to come to terms with them. To reach the level where we can perceive the whole, we have to be prepared to surrender ourselves. The affirmative and negative experiences and opportunities of a life are all one. Fundamentally, it is impossible to grasp something as having been beautiful before it was ugly, or joyful before it was miserable. Without a comparison, these concepts are impossible to express.

Who would believe that people are actually more fortunate than this thesis and antithesis would suggest? Rather than focusing on fortune, perhaps we should stress the importance of truly knowing what is of value in our lives, relishing the ability to feel and expressing gratitude for all that is. If we look at all life with love in our hearts, this joy knocks the door of hope ajar for us.

Psychology and psychiatry are two often-used resources for finding a resolution for spiritual problems. Despite their good efforts in trying to find the causes of these karmic disorders, additional assistance is sometimes necessary to resolve the karmic component of these illnesses. Essentially the Gestalt theory, in psychotherapeutic terms, is the acceptance of the spiritual body as well as all the other bodies—emotional, mental, etheric and physical—as a whole. Energy has the tendency in the emotional and mental bodies to first deconstruct and then reconstruct, whereas the spiritual body reflects events as a whole in the form of our super-ego. Our karma represents this wholeness. When there is an excess of unresolved mental imbalances in our karma, then the entire karma moves into a negative energy mode.

We must emphasize this: what concerns us in this dimension is not the health of the components, but of the whole. It does not matter how much we can load our emotional and mental bodies with love and equilibrium, if we have unresolved karma, we can never have sustained health. To resolve karmic issues we must look back, take stock of our past mistakes and reach a new level of maturity. As long as we fail to learn from these experiences and as long as we do not change our ways, the boomerang will continue to return, sending us sprawling each time.

To cleanse our karma we need to reflect on our negative experiences. If we have blamed others and held them responsible, we must replace our anger, accept our own faults and shortcomings and forgive everyone and everything, starting with ourselves. If we cannot forgive ourselves and others and even the events themselves, we will never find the road to love.

The spiritual body is connected to all the universes and it is the body that most affects the etheric body. As mentioned earlier, the etheric body acts like a power station; the electromagnetic energy is transmitted to the upper emotional, mental and spiritual bodies in vibrational waves and, once recoded, is reflected back to the etheric body. When we can understand this, any idea of the physical body being just a biochemical metabolic mechanism becomes redundant. As I have been careful to point out, it is not just the health of the physical body that must addressed; equally important is the health of the etheric, emotional, mental and spiritual bodies.

This is why treatment of disease by medication alone is not adequate. We also cannot disregard that the pharmaceutical treatment of many chronic diseases can even create the opposite effect to that which was intended. If there are blockages in the energy channels between the upper bodies and the physical body they will invariably leads to disorders in the organs as well as hormonal, neural, and metabolic disorders.

Methods used for the treatment of electrical (energy) blockages.

- Bio-electric resonance therapy
- Homeopathic resonance therapy
- Acupuncture energy channel therapy
- Matrix regeneration therapy (Connective tissue detoxification and renewal)
- Color and sound therapy (a therapy developed to modify the thought models of color and sound)
- Magnetic field therapy (realigning disorders in the body's magnetic field)

The function of bio-energy equipment is to diagnose and treat electrical blockages in our bodies. As we consider our other bodies as well as our physical body and the emphasis is on the health of the immune system, it might be timely to examine this equipment in more detail.

# VIII

# The Synthesis of Healthy Living and the Energy Values of the Human Conscious

Today we find ourselves on the cusp of a new understanding of a healthy life. We no longer regard our bodies as a mechanism of flesh, bone and chemical reactions. More of us have become conscious of our high energy bodies and the spiritual dimension. We are part of a movement, aware of the affirmative and negative effects to our physical, etheric, emotional, mental and spiritual bodies. But it is with regret that we note that despite all these developments, there are still very many physicians who view the human body as a complex piece of machinery. This is despite the many vibrational medicine practitioners of the Einstein paradigm who are achieving recognition in demonstrating that we are an interconnected network of energy fields and the cellular system.

Similarly, the many diagnostic and treatment methods that draw upon the Einstein paradigm are all branches of vibrational medicine. This is because it is a universal reality that the single feature that makes us human and the basic energy force are one and the same: vibration.

Vibrational medicine's modus operandi is quite clear: to use diagnoses or therapies that manipulate or stimulate the basic bodily vibrational order. The human body is a complex vibrational system where every cell, tissue and organ has its own specific vibrational frequency. This communication network within the bodily system continuously transmits every aspect of the individual's life. A perpetual cause and effect dialogue is carried out between the energy bodies and the physical body. Separating energy and matter is inconceivable, for in healthy cellular metabolism there is a ceaseless metamorphosis of energy into matter and matter into energy. As a result, it must be stressed that our bi-polar world evolved from photon energy or, put another way, from light.

This perpetual process of transformation merely demonstrates that matter is just the secondary form of energy. To put it in a different way, matter is energy's concentrated condition. We are able to affect matter by changing the frequencies in the energy fields. When energy transforms into matter it is separated into a photon energy particle, a negatively charged electron particle, a positively charged proton particle and the atom's nucleus in which the neutron is found. These three forces, the electron, proton and neutron, are within, and the reason behind, every ordinary and extraordinary event within the universe.

- The electron is the primary active force.
- The proton is the passive force.
- The neutron, as its name suggests, is neutral and is the stabilizing force.
- These three forces order both the physical and the high energy bodies.
- The active force of the electron drives the bodily systems.
- The positively charged proton is the reactive force, while the neutron is the balancing force of the energy systems.

Polar activity is found at both the functional and structural levels in the human organism. Examples of this include the relationship between the spiritual and physical bodies and between the polar meridians and the bodily organs. For every cause there is an effect. Every energy form communicates data when concentrated and polarized at the material configuration. Consider the operating system of the computer. For it to function correctly it must receive complete data that have been converted to code from letters and numbers. Code is created from electrical current producing two values: when the current flows "on" or "1,"; and when the current is "off" "0." This is called binary code. Every stroke of the keyboard produces binary code made up of these "ones" or "zeros" and all the data in the computer are stored or transmitted in this way.

Precisely the same situation exists with the energy of the positive "+" and negative "-" poles of our balance and rotation; this energy must be regarded as information or data transfer. Like computer code, the polarity balance of our bodies expresses itself in energy output. When a blockage occurs there are disruptions to the energy rotation that then hinder data transfer, causing issues to emerge. Polarity and the concept of opposing forces can also be expressed by what is called "Yin and Yang".

The theory of Yin-Yang expresses a basic law: Every entity in nature and the universe is interdependent. For anything to be wholly complete it must acknowledge its coexistence with its counterpart. Day is not complete without night; as one without the other becomes meaningless. The concept of Yin-Yang refers to the mutual transformation of opposite energy values and is not related to any specific religious belief.

When the poles are independent of each other, as in poor health conditions, only minute traces of each are found in the opposite pole. For this reason, physiognomy and psychology cannot be examined separately. Each organ has a Yin function and a Yang function. The kidney has Yin characteristics; which is why a condition originating from the kidneys exacerbates our phobias, making us cold and unstable. When these phobias exceed the limits of the body they take on Yang characteristics and become temperaments that enter the field of contemporary psychological analysis.

## Primary Yin / Yang principles

| Yin | Yang |
|---|---|
| Feminine | / Masculine |
| Water | / Fire |
| Cold | / Hot |
| Still | / Agitated |
| Contraction | / Expansion |
| Chronic | / Acute |
| Shortage | / Excess |
| Moon | / Sun |
| Night | / Day |
| Passive | / Active |
| Destructive | / Constructive |

Each is bipolar in opposition to one another.

As long as this situation persists, trying to establish equilibrium becomes a vicious circle. Everything is in a state of flux, in a dynamic process of motion and development. Transformation occurs within the bounds of its own process. In other words, transformation is realized whether harmoniously or not. Harmony in the Yin-Yang perspective must be at the stable levels, while disharmony will always be distanced from stability and equilibrium. While there is always a quest for stability and equilibrium, motion is perpetual. In acupuncture, the Yin-Yang of the healthy body are in harmony, while in ill health they are not.

As we have previously established, matter is both wave form and energy, displaying particle characteristics and a process of fusion; it is a quantum physics example of the coexistence of opposites. Ch'i is the word used to describe the life energy flow that brought Yin and Yang into existence. This brief description encompasses a number of interpretations. There is no concept of good or evil in Yin-Yang, only the acknowledgment of their existence. Using this perspective, we can deal with "negative" events calmly, as we have the tools to achieve harmony, overcome hardship or rein in upset.

Everything in the universe proceeds on the principle of polarity—as two opposite poles. Every life falls within these parameters, for good or for bad, fortunate or unfortunate, beautiful or ugly. It is up to us to remain aware that to be always thankful for beauty and good fortune. If we can achieve this we can only invite more fortune, beauty and good into our lives. From the holistic perspective we are obliged to regard different levels of existence as a whole. The same principle applies to ill health: we must approach diagnosis and treatment from a bi-polar perspective. While examining energy disorders of the upper energy bodies we must similarly be considering any cellular disorders of the physical body.

A healthy existence is a quest for synthesis; we must research, using the laws of polar activity, what the function of active, passive and neutral forces signify to the human organism. Following this, we need to form the synthesis of healthy living from the thesis and antithesis of the relationship between the bodies' energy levels and the elements that form opposing interconnections. Synthesis refers to the consolidation of thesis and antithesis. To examine the details of these two components, it is helpful to examine what the hidden intimations of human behavior reveal.

How can we achieve harmony with the subconscious elements of our higher energy bodies and the conscious of our physical body?

## The energy values of the human conscious

After many years of research into the human conscious, Dr David R. Hawkins published the results of the equivalents in energy values in his book *Power vs. Force*. Referring to them will help understand the concept of harmony that we have just discussed. Dr. Hawkins' research revealed seventeen levels of the conscious. These start with those displaying the highest energy levels and move down to those with the lowest.

## The 17 levels of the conscious as determined by Dr. Hawkins are:

- Revelation
- Willingness
- Fear
- Contentment
- Impartiality
- Grief
- Joy
- Courage
- Indifference
- Love
- Egoism
- Blame
- Reason
- Anger
- Shame
- Approval
- Desire

It may be appropriate to provide a brief analysis before proceeding to the details of these components, which will form the basis of our understanding of bodily synthesis. But first, let us consider these sage words:

- Life is difficult.
- Because your happiness depends on other people, life is a series of problems. Problems are life.
- Do you want to complain about this or resolve it?
- Happiness is a journey not a destination.
- There is no road leading to happiness; happiness is the road itself.
- Life is a short journey in this world, enjoy it.
- All the bodies, including the physical one, are energy.
- The most important thing is the soul. The worldly journey begins and ends in this world. The soul is endless energy and never dies.
- The human life processes are controlled both bio-physically and by a continuous stream of information.
- Our physical body has two principal energy sources, bio-electricity and magnetic field energy.
- The important thing is not to heal a disorder's symptoms but to relieve its real causes.

- Youth is a testament to human courage whereas old age is the result of fear.
- Always live for the moment and be full of love.
- The applause always dies. Awards, cups and medals inevitably gather dust. Those who once wore crowns are one day soon forgotten. But if a candle lights another candle, nothing is ever lost of the illumination it passes on.

With this understanding we must return ourselves to the point where the sole purpose of life is to leave behind a light, a light of love, a light of equilibrium and the light of our Creator.

Taking into account the conscious components of Dr. Hawkins, and without forgetting synthesis and the bodily energy values, let us move on to greater familiarity with the thesis, antithesis and neutral powers of the high energy bodies, namely those of the emotional, mental and spiritual bodies. And let us list the levels of their energy values.

## The emotional body's synthesis

First, let us consider the emotional body. When listed in order of energy levels this body's conscious elements are thus: joy, love, courage, ego, anger and indifference. The highest energy level is "joy." Joy is elation. One feels joy when something long yearned for is achieved, or for something that gives great pleasure. Joy is like flying. What we are trying to demonstrate is which among all those components that affect the body represents the thesis or antithesis of the elements of the conscious. Our purpose is to determine each of the body's thesis and antithesis components. However confident Dr. Hawkins may be in placing joy above love on the energy scale, one thing is clear—that the long run, love has the potential for the greatest energy level.

A dictionary definition of love could be: "Love is an emotion that describes one person's close attention, interest and attachment to another person or thing." It is possible for us to be always full of love, but not always full of joy. If only we could be! We have to accept that this goes against the nature of our creation. For this reason we are able to use "love" as a thesis element in our emotional body. So, if love is the thesis, what could be the antithesis for the love energy component?

In Dr. Hawkins" list, the energy value of "courage" is higher than that of "egotism." But if we measure them in terms of opposition, "egoism" comes out ahead. We should be aware that the concept of egotism can also define an ability for self-preservation and holding oneself in high esteem. Naturally, this type of self-confidence must be tempered with the capability for self-love, so that the result can be positive rather than negative. It is in this sense that we address it here. Therefore we can take egoism as our antithesis. However, we must not overlook its more common definition, meaning "extremely self-centered; a taker, not a giver; full of oneself; arrogant, pompous and boastful." If we cannot be in control of ourselves we will always find love difficult to find. Anyone who has an inflated opinion of themselves will find it difficult to do anything for others and even courage will be in short supply.

We have established that for the emotional body the thesis is love and the antithesis is egoism; that for the emotional body the stimulus for health is "love" and the power of resistance comes from "egoism." Now we must establish the neutral force that holds these two in equilibrium. It is possible, using "indifference" from the emotional body's conscious elements, to hold egotism in check. Egotism and self-centeredness are extremely powerful components but indifference is capable of limiting them. Indifference is very similar to apathy, which is the ability to withhold emotions and interest in anything.

The players are clear: active power is "love;" the passive power is "egotism" and the neutral power is "indifference." The healthy synthesis of the emotional body consists of love and egotism together, with egotism being bound by indifference. In this case, synthesis and synergy are synonymous as the two elements are the thesis of love and the antithesis of egoism.

## The mental body's synthesis

There are five components in the organization of the consciousness of the mental body. Dr Hawkins places "reason" at the top of the list; following are approval, willingness, impartiality and fear. In examining the five, we see that "reason" is our active force; "fear" our opposing force; and "willingness" our neutral force. Willingness can also be defined as volition. In terms of balance, individuals who exhibit volition can conquer their fears.

The healthy life synthesis of the mental body is thus: The thesis is "reason"; "fear" is the antithesis; and "willingness" becomes our neutral power. One of our most defining aspects is our ability to overcome fear. If we truly wish to overcome our fears and keep balance in our lives, we must develop the ability to examine, in a healthy way, the reasons for those fears. A person who is capable of this, and of conquering their fear, will find themselves filled with love and well balanced.

As a direct result of being full of love and being able to love ourselves, our capacity for loving others increases and we conquer fear. We can now understand the meaning of universal love. If we are obsessed or have groundless phobias, troubles or sorrows—but above all fear, we have two golden keys to ridding ourselves of these: love and balance. These two will open the locked doors of the physical and energy bodies.

## The spiritual body's synthesis

Let us now consider the health of the spiritual body. The conscious elements of the spiritual body can be listed in this way: revelation, contentment, grief, desire, blame and shame. Energy is at its highest in the spiritual body and its most active power comes from the "source." The "source" is called many names: the Creator, Jehovah, God or Allah, to name but a few. As the spiritual body is the closest to the cosmos, it takes on a role as the "resource" body. The spiritual body is at the same time our Gestalt body: The sum of the parts is greater than the whole.

All our thoughts, physical, emotional or mental in origin, are recorded in the "black box" of our spiritual body as karma. This body has an elevated awareness of the "source" thus our karma is loaded with positive energy. This can be interpreted as "contentment." Thus, what Dr. Hawkins chose to call contentment, we will refer to as the "source."

Sad but true: we find that it is difficult for someone without faith to be content. It would seem that faith, simply on its own, brings contentment. If we survey our lives we see that this point of triangulation is always the "source."

Death is one of life's two certainties: we all die. The other certainty, whether or not we believe in life after death, is that the "source" is, and always will be, our Creator. The source of contentment is the "source." Thus, the spiritual body's active power is "contentment" and its passive power is "blame." Blame in the spiritual body is a karmic disorder, a karmic disease. The most effective way to counter karmic disease is through faith.

The powers of "contentment" and "blame" are balanced out by the neutral power of revelation. Perhaps you wonder how the antithesis of "contentment" can be "blame." Those that cannot believe in a Creator will consistently experience issues with contentment, as well as with comprehending love and equilibrium. Without love and equilibrium it is nearly impossible to draw near to the Creator. Generally it seems that people with love and balance issues are the same ones who blame others, whether family, friends, co-workers or society in general.

With this sort of emptiness in a life—it makes no difference if developments are positive or not—the individual will inevitably become aimless. When confronted with difficulties, they will be quick to blame. As they blame others so generously, the subconscious makes its own rightful claim. It is when such individuals look in the mirror, that they will come to understand where blame rightfully belongs.

The antithesis of "contentment" is "blame;" and atheists are faced with an issue of balance as they have no point of reference. The unbalanced will always try blaming others. This is why we can extend the antithesis from blame to include guilt.

Enlightened individuals always have an advanced level of awareness. The enlightened are always people of faith. At minimum, they have faith in themselves and in humanity. The synthesis of the spiritual body is: thesis, "contentment"; antithesis, "blame" and the neutral power, "revelation." Those of faith and the enlightened have the ability to overcome the passive power of "blame" and to possess a healthy spiritual body.

# IX

# The Significance of Love

## Thought is energy; therefore, life is thought

Almost everyone has heard of Einstein's groundbreaking quantum physics formula, $E=MC^2$. But how many of us understand it? We are probably just happy to know that energy is equal to matter multiplied by the square of the speed of light. But to think, to research, and to ponder that everything in existence is concealed within this equation requires responsibility and time. It does not require anything like a quantum leap, though, to comprehend that this is the same formula as the law of "energy equaling matter."

While concentrated energy in the form of light and matter can be seen by the naked eye, the energy waves of the complex network of high frequency energy that surrounds the universe cannot be detected by any of the five senses; just as the ear cannot detect sound at frequencies below and beyond its range. Each one of us is nothing more than a ball of energy. The atoms that compose our body while alive release a ball of photon energy or electromagnetic radiation when we die.

And where does that energy go? With all the advances in technology we still have no scientific evidence to determine the destination. Esoteric thinkers believe that the spirit goes to an unknown place called "spatiom."

If we study religious texts we see that different civilizations at different times in history have extensive literature on life after death. Scientifically we have not been able to determine what happens to us when we die. But returning to Einstein, we see from his formula that energy cannot be destroyed. Thus, it stands to reason that we, being composed of energy, cannot be destroyed. Descriptions of the after-life frequently appear in religious texts, but we lack evidence of it from any living human.

We are considering these points to emphasize how thought is also energy and why it is imperative to try to understand its effects. In our age the extraordinary power of thought has been confirmed by science and we come across many examples in press and television. For example, the case of the quadriplegic who can control and use a computer with only his brain: How is this possible? It takes place by using sophisticated electronics and a trained thought mechanism.

There is a polarity to the order and balance of the universe; it is a force that is in "plus" or "minus" mode. The body's right side up to the neck is plus, while the left is minus. The right half of the head is plus and the left minus. The etheric body sustains this polarity with a bioelectric current. By tensing or relaxing his thought signals, the quadriplegic can send an electrical signal to a connected, configured computer and make it function. If thought has such power, imagine the quality of the health and strength of someone with a consistently affirmative outlook, compared to an individual with a consistently negative outlook.

Even when posited as hypothesis, the immune system of a positive thinker is perceived as stronger than that of a negative thinker. Most of us are familiar words like these: "Our thoughts shape our actions, our actions our nature, our nature our character, our character our lives." To put it briefly, if we want to live healthily we must think healthily! If we think healthily and positively, our actions, our nature, our character and our lives will be irreversibly affected for the better. Life is thought for our thoughts lead to our actions and we become our actions.

# Considerations about loving ourselves

Before delving into detail, let us approach love from a different perspective. The basic understanding of loving is a thought—energy—and thus a product of a vibrational frequency. For instance, the answer to "What is the secret of a good marriage?" could be "Become what you hold in common." In human relationships it is now trendy to discuss chemistry or electricity. This is very close to scientific truth.

When two people are attracted to each other their vibrational frequencies, or those frequencies' composition, are similar. This creates a biological resonance event. If the thoughts of two individuals are of the same vibrational frequency mode, there is a strong probability that eye contact will reveal a powerful empathy. As wirelesses on the same frequency communicate with each other, so do human beings. Communication and understanding become easier. And within time this relationship has a chance of evolving into love.

There is another theory—that opposites attract—but very often these relationships are like a quick burst of flame that degenerate rapidly into scorched earth. Sustaining this sort of relationship is difficult. A lasting relationship will include common beliefs, while similarities of vibrational frequencies enable harmony and turn it into love. The same is true of our communication with ourselves. If, when we look into the mirror our vibrational frequency is the same as our reflection, we can look at ourselves with affection. We can be aware of aches or pains in our body. In this case when we look in the mirror we will be concentrating on the negative, on a fault or a shortcoming, and then there is no way we can claim that we were viewing ourselves with affection.

If loving ourselves were only as easy as saying "I love you!" Beginning from infancy, we are molded by a lifetime of thought and experience. This includes learning right from wrong, systems of ethics, and so on. Our society and everything that happens around us has a direct impact on our subconscious, where it is stored in the "black box" of our karma. Because of these messages, even articulating "loving ourselves" can sound alien to our ears.

The first reaction might be, "Loving myself? How egotistical is that?" Or we might hear: "Love your family and your country first, for who will benefit from loving yourself?" This line of thought derives from the result, not from the cause; in trying to change the result, those who believe this way fail to try to understand the cause. If we accept one of the most important aspects of life to be the pursuit of happiness, then we must ask ourselves this question: "If I am not happy, how can I expect my family, my loved ones and others to be happy?"

The road to happiness is through loving oneself. Those who truly succeed in loving themselves are more inclined to love others. Naturally, those who love themselves with the energy of positive thought will find that they are directed to living better, more productively and with greater health; with the feeling that they deserve it. This empowers them to sustain healthy self–love. We begin this process gradually—taking the first steps, then, with strength and confidence gained from practice, we reach our goal.

Have no regrets about the past. Do not be anxious about the future and seek out the best way to love yourself.

## What we have to do to love ourselves

To be able to love ourselves we must first be open, transparent, confident and balanced. "No man is an island." We all have an inner and an outer self and it is essential to keep these two aspects in equilibrium.

If we analyze our lives from our childhood to the present, we begin the process of balancing our inner and outer worlds. Our success in achieving this balance affects our ability to be happy and full of love. For many of us, our lives have been about marketing ourselves—"brand me." We were born and, to make sure we were fed, we gurgled for our mother's pleasure. At school, we worked to persuade our teachers to perceive us as good, hardworking students so we could get the grades we wanted. While we are on the subject, did we not behave in a similar fashion when seeking a romantic partner? In our work life, do we not market ourselves for our boss or for our clients? The years progress and when our lives are drawing to an end, we consider marketing ourselves to a Being that might have some influence in our eternal lives. Perhaps we start to embellish our speech with religious motifs and become more aware of the spiritual sensitivities.

But if we are already leading a balanced existence with our outer world, we find ourselves automatically drawn to that which is beautiful and harmonious without resorting to self-marketing. With this harmony, we can be happy in the knowledge that we have proceeded a long way toward loving ourselves.

Now to examine the balance between our inner and outer worlds.

According to the celebrated American psychologist, Abraham Maslow, there are five conditions for happiness. Listed in order of importance they are:

**Maslow's five conditions for happiness**
- Having enough to eat
- Security
- Having emotional needs met
- Proving one's worth
- Working in a job we like and realizing our potentials

Health should be included in the concept of security; without health, it is impossible to move up the happiness table. Perhaps success could be included but if there are issues with emotional needs then we may believe that this is our path to happiness. As can be understood, "loving oneself" is a difficult task to accomplish.

Loving ourselves, maintaining a balance between our inner and outer worlds and happiness are concepts that are bound to the way we think. Remember that thought is energy, "Which way of thinking do we have?" is a question that requires careful consideration. If it appears that our thoughts are usually negative, then we still work to do.

Negative thinking is no different than a dangerous disease. In time, negative thoughts block the body's energy channels and unbalance the body's metabolic regulation. A build-up of toxins will cripple the organism's healthy vibrational frequencies, leaving cells exposed to potential inflammation and degeneration. In extreme cases, if left unchecked, this can lead to cancer. If certain types of cancer are examined from a vibrational medicine perspective, their principle cause will be shown to stem from stress.

But just commencing positive thought is not enough to correct a negative condition that needs attention. If you have a mole on your body that is growing, it does not matter how positively you concentrate on correcting the innate negativity, the mole will remain unaffected. This is because there is a suspicion about that mole gnawing at your consciousness and removing any possibility of sustained positive thought. Positive thought obtains its strength from doing what is right and necessary. That growing mole should be shown to a doctor but as we do this, and every stage that follows, we must reinforce ourselves with positive affirmation that everything is going to be all right.

Returning to Maslow's happiness table, if our stomachs are full, our concern becomes security; if we are secure, we move to belonging and giving and receiving love. If we have those, it becomes about proving ourselves and then becoming content in what we do. However, all these concerns are only possible with positive thought. A fascinating aspect of Maslow's happiness table is that those at the "having enough to eat" level probably do not even consider if they are happy or not. Generally it is those at the 'success" levels who have greater dissatisfaction with their level of happiness and are looking for more.

Perhaps this is how "ignorance is bliss" originated. Basically: to get the energy of positive thought, we must approach everything differently. As we start to ascend within the Maslow happiness table, we must grasp every moment in a positive way and live in happiness at whatever level we find ourselves. Almost every situation can be overcome with positively balanced thought and love. In short, the infra-structure for loving others and happiness is to love ourselves.

We must carefully nurture the soil to plant harmony between our inner and outer worlds and for love and happiness to grow and bloom. We have all encountered injustice, hurt, disappointment and sorrow at some point. Life is not fair—or rather, that is the perception—and it is definitely not easy; many people are victims of injustice. Despite these experiences, and instead of dwelling on the past, we must constructively and positively look forward, the first step in positive thought.

Positive thinking, like any newly acquired skill, requires consistent repetition of the first steps and is strengthened by short thinking exercises. Each day we must start by directing our thoughts to positive and constructive; before long, we will see that positive thinking is automatic. Following is a balanced harmony, and then, bounding towards creativity, happiness and love can only ensue.

## The ways of reasoning

There is an intimate relationship between the way we reason and resonance energy. For the majority of humanity, making a decision depends on a lifetime's accumulation of what is considered to be right, and then viewing it from that perspective.

Few people have the ability to approach decision making from different perspectives, but this is the only way forward, the only way to break out of our conditioned way of decision making and to think freely.

According to research conducted on the way we reason, we are conditioned both by nature and by nurture, by our social environment and even by our nationality and religious beliefs. In my book, *The Art of Being Happy and Successful*, I used an example from research conducted in the United States at the end of the 1980s. The findings divided the way we reason into five distinct categories.

### The Ways People Reason

- Synthesis thought
- Realist thought
- Analytic thought
- Idealist thought
- Pragmatist thought

These different types of reasoning have strong and weak aspects. This study revealed that sixty-five percent of the subjects possessed a single strategic approach to their thinking, while the remaining thirty-five percent had an approach similar to a chess player, with different stages and possibilities in their thought processes.

Let us examine these five main groups individually.

### Synthesis thought

Those who engage in synthesis thought approach almost every subject by searching for new and original aspects to combine. A favorite approach of synthesists is to collect and evaluate different ideas. Synthesists will often ask themselves: "If I take two opposing ideas and combine them, what is the result?" "If" is a constant refrain, as they hypothesize various combinations of ideas and information.

We often find that it is the synthesists who investigate subjects ignored by others, in an effort to reveal more than one possibility. But it is hard to find a single solution when working with sythesists. Synthesists always take on opposing ideas to produce the appropriate solution. But as synthesists are always dealing with hypotheses they have a resistance to reality and find it hard to accept. They demonstrate this reaction by overusing "if," "but" and "but if." While generally calm, synthesists can display strong reactions to opinions they are unable to accept. But they are masterful definers of different aspects of any given concept. They appear to be deeply skeptical and can give the impression of being argumentative. They enjoy intellectual subjects like philosophy and other speculative topics but avoid the mundane.

## Realist thought

In general, realists and pragmatists have a similar style of deliberation. These two groups can overlap but they have some significant differences. These are most evident in their approach to hypotheses and judgments. Realists pursue concrete evaluation while pragmatists will choose appraisal over experience, bringing them closer to the analyst way of thinking. Realists will immediately demonstrate whether they accept a subject or not. Their favorite expression is "As everyone knows…." They usually express their argument positively and in a controlled manner. They like to express their opinions on subjects that are brief, to the point and can be backed up with data. They find emotional or hypothetical topics boring.

## Analytic thought

Analytic thinkers approach questions and problems carefully, logically and methodically. Before making a decision they will collect as much data as possible and make a detailed analysis.

Analytic thinkers have a theory for almost everything. They yearn to see the world as rational, logical and well ordered. For every problem they will attempt to devise a methodology or formula. Above all they want to be certain of events and any possible outcomes. Analytic thinkers are invariably unemotional and hard to comprehend. Their favorite expression is: "Looking at it logically..." They express themselves in a dry, careful and self-controlled manner. They do not like pointless, illogical and/or speculative conversation. They feel uncomfortable under stress and have a tendency to diverge from the subject.

## Idealist thought

Idealist thinkers generally take a broad view. They are forward looking and purposeful. Often they ask: "Where are we going and why?" They are interested in both society and the individual. They are interested in innovation and in social values. Like sythesists, idealist thinkers usually focus on things more precious than reality and they are often skeptical of complicated facts. Idealist thinker's philosophy of life can be summed up thus: "Doing right or attempting to do right is its own greatest reward." Idealist thinkers are careful and tend to be accepting, conciliatory and warm-hearted. They often ask: "Do you really think like that?" They express their feelings and opinions openly. They express themselves in a hopeful, enquiring manner and they take pleasure in concerning themselves with the problems of others. They are givers and have little time for conversations about materialism, but their motivation can suffer when they are under stress.

## Pragmatist thought

Beginning with the precept, "thought is energy", let us look into which of these five methods of thought can increase the body's energy and provide us with the healthiest perspective. Of the five ways of thinking, the pragmatist thinker comes closer than any of the others. Pragmatist thinkers approach the subject or problem in a series of stages and try to resolve it by giving the clearest outcome. Unlike the synthesists, they do not show a strong reaction to what they consider an unacceptable situation. They are not skeptical and neither do they delve into philo- sophical or speculative opinions. They demonstrate an approach that does not just focus on the problem but on the solution and its outcome.

Unlike the analytical thinkers' approach, with every detail of the solution considered, the pragmatist thinker searches for a practical, applicable solution. The pragmatist thinker is open- minded, social and has a good sense of humor. Pragmatist thinkers, even under stress, try to get to the solution, where analytical thinkers may become distracted from the subject.

Pragmatist thinkers, just like the realist ones, are not inter- ested in material success. They know that they must find a definitive resolution for every issue and unlike the realist thinker they take an interest in subjects that appear to be hypothetical. They are always ready and willing to find a pos- itive solution to negative situations. They often suggest a solu- tion-based approach: "Come on, let's find a mutual solution together."

Idealist and pragmatist thinkers have much in common but their differences are equally striking. For example, idealist thinkers generally concentrate their views on the merits of a subject rather than the facts. They are skeptical of subjects that are obscure and they can become fragile when under stress. The stereotype of the idealist thinker is the bleeding heart; none of these characteristics are found in the pragmatist thinker.

This study was done many years ago and it is difficult to say whether a new study would reveal different results; how- ever, with the present understanding it is unlikely. But if the study were done in a different country from the United States, what then are the chances of different results? It is accepted that behavior patterns can be very similar but thought processes could reveal differences. It is more than likely that the situation internationally would be far more complex than five basic methods of thinking. Many of us might believe that our thinking patterns combined more than one of the attributes of the table. Perhaps to isolate a dominant thinking type might be a better approach after all. But one thing is clear, these types of analysis, even as generalizations go a long way to help us understand ourselves and the societies in which we live.

It is important for us to study which thinking method best serves us in positively affecting the physical and etheric bodies and provides them with the healthiest vibrational energy, which is our most pressing concern. We should not try to squeeze ourselves into the attributes of the pragmatist thinker, but instead ask ourselves "What is the best path for me?" If we remain "topped up" with positive thought energy, it really makes little difference to which group of thinker we feel we belong.

Let me reiterate, most important is the state of the levels of our vibrational energy frequencies. As much as the pragmatist way of thinking may seem the most constructive, negative aspects of the other ways of thinking can always be turned to positive advantage. Even with different approaches to thinking, it is possible to be positive and harness the energy of healthy vibration because the power of thought is a powerful energy source.

## Universal love begins with loving oneself

The desire to love ourselves is the precursor to universal love. In his book, *Mind into Matter*, Prof. Fred Alan Wolf lists four actions we should learn by heart to achieve our desires. The four actions that Prof. Wolf encourages us to learn are, to think, to feel, to be moved and to perceive.

Prof. Wolf proposes that when we become time we allow ourselves to be moved with the flow like a river, "When we flow with the river, the river suddenly loses all the violent currents we viewed from the bank and becomes silent and as though motionless, we lose any sense of time because we have become time.

The void comes about by "feeling," and the feelings described here are the electrons or other electrically charged particles that move from one point to another. Our basic emotions describe the transformation into energy that comes about when the "feeling" electrons, moving in the void, are ionized and turned into energy.

As for movement, Prof. Wolf describes how the changes that develop from thought are turned into perception that plays a pivotal role in achieving our desires. In other words, perception boosts the power of our desire and sets it in motion.

In short, what Prof. Wolf is saying is that "our perception has the capacity to define where we are going and what we are doing." This suggests that an individual's affirmations can achieve resonance acceleration. We could also say that the road to "loving ourselves" begins with answering our desires using these four actions. We can hone the power of our perception by whichever action can turn our affection to ourselves, by thinking, feeling or by being moved.

Thus, whatever deep, burning desire we might possess will respond to the power of vibrational potential energy and open up the gates of universal love for all of us. Even the word love has its own energy. There are very few objectives this universal energy cannot achieve, at least too few to mention. Love is a word with a high vibrational frequency and effect. The old proverb could never be closer to the truth: "Sweet words will even draw the snake from its lair."

People who cannot love themselves cannot love others, and to love ourselves we must first know ourselves. To achieve this we must continually analyze ourselves, as a psychologist does, and develop the capacity to evaluate ourselves. This is of paramount importance. Those who lack affection for themselves will not be able to love the rest of humanity; equally they cannot look with love upon their "loved" ones, and friends. Thus, let us approach the subject like a psychologist and ask ourselves a few searching questions.

- Generally speaking, am I happy with myself?
- Do I hold others responsible for things that happen to me or do I turn the blame on myself?
- Am I able to forgive myself and others?
- Am I at peace with myself and others?
- Am I always myself or am I like a great actor, always concealing my true identity?
- Do I find myself truly honest?
- Do I respect myself?
- Do I trust myself?
- Do I have a sufficient foundation of self-confidence?

The answers to these questions will be helpful in understanding ourselves, our behavior, our habits and our tendencies. We must make time to know ourselves, as most of the time we are still too frightened to look into our inner self and confront the real persona. If that is the case, we must waste no time and start to get to know ourselves right now. This is because our fears are in our sub-conscious and if we can come face-to-face with them, it will go a long way to eliminating them forever.

First, we must accept ourselves for who we are and begin to analyze all the characteristics of ourselves we do not like and confront those fears. It is our responsibility. If we leave it to others to appraise and criticize us, we will never get to know our real selves. To leave this responsibility to others is like leaving our personal freedom in someone else's hands.

Let us not be frightened of revealing our weaknesses; if we can find the courage to do this, believe me when I say that that then we are more than halfway to achieving our goal. When we become knowledgeable about ourselves we will be amazed by how much of us that is good, virtuous and beautiful. The point of this effort is to reveal our real worth. It is not to impress or prove something about our value to others. We should remain aware that if we give importance and value to the opinions of others before our own, we will never be able to love ourselves in the true sense of the word.

The vital point here is not how we appear to others, neither is it how much money we have nor what we do; it is who we are. This is because our short stay on the mortal coil should be one of growth and change. Happiness can, and should, increase as we become older.

The sociologist Yang Yang, of the University of Chicago's National Opinion Research Center, published the results of a 32-year survey conducted between 1972 and 2004 concerning the relationship between happiness and ageing. It was perceived that we are all inclined to develop over a period of time. The greatest mistake that we can make is to look at the temporary physical superiority of youth and be misled about our true identity. When we realize who we really are, we become aware that the only real power is that which is within us.

There is no secret to living, but the secret of life is to live knowing ourselves. The way to reach this state passes through the realization of who we are. This can be done by the remote personalization of our infatuations and premonitions. This personalization can be done by asking ourselves a few questions:

- What are my positive and negative sides?
- What are my strong and weak characteristics?
- Do I have habits that I can list in order of their good and bad aspects?
- Do I have any obsessions?
- What are my physical, mental, emotional and spiritual complaints?
- Am I an honest person in terms of society's value system?
- Was there "loyal friendship" in the good things that I have done for myself?
- How much importance do I place on material values?

The list of questions could be even longer. Evaluating the answers can reveal important clues as to how much an individual knows about him or herself, while at the same time providing a personality profile. If we can honestly and bravely assess the resulting profile, we will have a detailed self-portrait in our hands. But to make this appraisal there are first some important principles to be considered.

The most significant of those principles is not to fall in the trap of thinking: "What does he or she have that I don't have?" Never get into an argument about anything. Never be concerned about what others have or do not have in the way of physical or non-physical assets. Of primary importance is that everyone is at peace with him or herself and to find inner contentment. To think of yourself as superior in "this or that" to someone else will only give a fleeting satisfaction. If this becomes habitual, it can create permanent dissatisfaction, as we will always confront people more talented than we. In the final analysis, everyone's talents and weaknesses are different and each individual must seek and discover their own personal pre-eminence. This is why we must throw out all comparisons and concentrate on seeing ourselves as we really are. We can only compete with ourselves. We must concentrate on accepting our shortcomings and weaknesses and then start seeing how we can correct them. Everything starts with modest steps, but if those first few paces are on the right road, we will see that we have covered a considerable distance in learning to love ourselves, because this is a race where there is only one competitor.

The second principle is not to fall into the error of having an unconditional belief in what others might have to say about our problems. We should explore every opportunity to read all we can about positive thinking from psychological and philosophical sources. This will direct us with the purpose of opening the path to love by understanding ourselves as well as others. We will discover ideas that will enlighten us, as well as introducing us to different points of view. However, bearing all this in mind, we must always listen to ourselves first. This is important because we know that allowing anyone to enter our psychological and emotional world and make suggestions on our behalf is fraught with difficulty. Of course, if there are deep rooted problems, professional help should never be ignored. But whatever the problem might be, we are the only person that can really put ourselves on the road to good health.

The final principal is to achieve a habitual state of thinking and act in equilibrium. From time to time, being at the extreme edge is part of human nature and part of the process of change. However, love that is sustainable and fulfilled with contentment is not to be found at the extreme; seeking out equilibrium is the far more realistic approach.

This principle is a guide for all stages of our lives; the direction is one we decide for ourselves on life's journey. As we continue to discover ourselves and sincerely account for all our shortcomings and mistakes we will see that our path takes us in the direction of everything that is good, beautiful and just which will bring into our lives evolution, development and progression. A few steps taken each day on the right path constitute the ideal groundwork for loving ourselves as we look forward to a love filled life with happiness a goal but, without ever forgetting how long that journey is.

# Love and balance

Without love we are only left with selfishness. Without love there is an imbalance in our energy reserves. In my opinion, the most apt description of those who see themselves as above everyone, as flawless and who are extreme egoists and narcissists is "little people." They might be swimming in money and fame, they might be in a position of political power and authority, but it would be pointless to try to fit the description of a "member of humanity" on their pampered frames. If they only knew that all we humans really want is health, contentment, success and happiness.

Without making a transcendental shift, psychological health becomes challenged and being a balanced human being becomes difficult. We have witnessed those who are crippled by being unable to either give or receive love, those who murmur under their breaths the two extremes of sanity: "I am the master of the universe" and "What am I?" The storm that rages inside them is an invitation to derangement.

At the other end of the scale are those who have been crushed by fear. For some, fear is introduced at the most important time in a child's development, 0-7 years. We start falling into the traps that are so carefully laid for the unsuspecting, fears that can scar us for life. Everyone has a different set of fears instilled in us by our family and environment; we take them with us throughout life. Though it is wrong, how often do we hear, "You're a child; you're too young to understand," or "Children should be seen, not heard." The erroneous thinking that lies behind this is that to be an adult means to be powerful and important. This attitude is used to process the minds of the young into longing for status and false respect that power without responsibility so often brings.

This is something that borders on a phobia. It becomes irrelevant if you are happy in work and life; but what many want to know is if you are powerful and earn a lot of money. As it appears that we have no authority to make our own decisions, fear becomes habitual and we bow our heads in resignation. These misinformed values are rooted early into the immature brains of the young. If we do not know how to think, how are we going to question our own existence, how are we going to make an evaluation? Freedom of thought is necessary and without freedom one cannot think freely. Without freedom there will be no free will and without that, how can lasting love ever develop?

An absence of love is an invitation for selfishness which, like fear, thrives on imbalance. Whatever the age and whatever the reason, fear drives us to imbalance and the inability to love. A lasting love must be built on a foundation of equilibrium. Life is a game of balance and the universal rule of creation is equilibrium. In moments of duress, nature's conceptualized forces will resist, delayed from the action necessary to maintain equilibrium. The two extremes are revealed in those who are as far from equilibrium as they are from love; on one hand there are those who display superiority complexes, narcissism and cynicism while taking pleasure in expressing their flowery condescension. And then there are those with inferiority complexes, so riddled with phobias that they virtually worship the powerful.

The concepts of balance and love are what make humanity worthy. Rumi had these telling words to say:

> So many people I have seen without a stitch of
> clothing on them
>
> So many clothes I have seen without a
> person in them.

If we connect someone who is without love and equilibrium to vibrational diagnosis equipment and measure their stress levels, we would see the turbulence of their inner worlds. If we look at the people around us and measure them by the criteria just mentioned, we see that many of them can be described as "little people," purely because of the lack of love in their lives.

Analyzing them still further, we would see that their concerns lie solely with what benefits them, either from a false position of superiority or from one of inferiority, both displaying self-ishness and lack of equilibrium. Because they are unable to love themselves they are unable to love or be loved in return. The pursuit of "power" becomes the most important thing in their lives whether the power of money, the material or status. How this power is used becomes the defining characteristic for the "little people" and the "members of humanity." Our lodestone must always be the concept of equilibrium. Everyone has that power whether they are rich or poor, regardless of social status.

The only real and effective power is the energy of love. The reality of what we have referred to in this book as the resonance principle is just that.

## How do we become a loving person?

How we become a loving person is directly linked to how much we can love ourselves. Those that do not love and are not at peace with themselves will find it nearly impossible to experience love in any form. We must attempt to change our perspective from "How do I look in the mirror" to "How do I look at the mirror?" The significant point here is not to wait passively to be loved by others, but to develop the habit of looking at all with love. We must accept that it is the art of giving, not the art of taking, that leads us to become loving persons.

While discussing altruism I would like to mention a book by Dr. Mustafa Merter called *Nine Hundred Storied People*. The book covers metaphysics and the psychology of the super-ego, but it was the chapter on "Good Works Therapy" that caught my eye. The title of the book is taken from an address by Rumi in his *Mesnevi*:

> Dearest friend! You are not alone; you are just part of the order of things! You are a deep and wide ocean. Oh enlightened one! Your extraordinary presence, it is perhaps nine

hundred storied, the depth as of a shoreless ocean, with hundreds of worlds having been swallowed up in that self same sea.

As Dr. Merter elaborates on the benefits and application of the "Good Works Therapy," he provides an example of a charitable organization called "Dosteli" ("Hand of Friendship") based in the city of Konya, Turkey. Dosteli also operates elsewhere in Turkey and in some developing countries. Among others of its works, this organization has started "Good Works" supermarkets, whereby the members of the organization visit and draw up a list of "customers." These customers are poor families struggling to feed themselves. The families are given a monthly quota of basic foodstuffs that they can obtain free from the supermarket. The suppliers who have signed up for the scheme also print a special barcode on the products so that a record can be kept of which product is going to which family. On the top floor of the supermarket is a clothing section where garments are donated by manufacturers who have a production surplus. The families can obtain free clothes twice a year.

Those involved in the organization donate their time and materials to families in need, all in the name of altruism. They could be described as silent anonymous angels. Dr. Merter notes that there is nothing patronizing, arrogant or boastful about the volunteers and they come from all walks of life. They come when they can, during their free time and on weekends, and do whatever job is assigned to them.

The significance of this is that it indicates a 180 degree shift to our existence and, in addition to the freedom this brings, without even realizing it we have come to the top floor of that nine-hundred story structure of human enlightenment. Dr. Merter calls this process of elevation "breaking free to the beyond;" that is to say, breaking the invisible membranes that bind us and, he continues, "is stepping out into a brighter more spacious world of reality."

We cannot remain unmoved by this or by other accounts of ordinary people coming together for the love of humankind. These constitute perfect examples of how being filled with love depends on how much we give, not on how much we take. Unfortunately there are too many people who devote much of their lives to the struggle of being able to take it all; and too many who dismiss those who do practice the art of giving. For such people, unconditional love is not even a concept; there must always be something to gain. While some are open to the love they give, there are others who lack patience and perseverance and are distraught by not receiving anything in return. They come to the conclusion that love does not pay. I wish they only knew that there is not a door that love cannot open.

If we can grasp the significance of quantum philosophy, then we must accept the incredible power of love. Where thought is energy, the very highest level of vibrational energy that can dramatically affect the frequencies and the subtle energy levels of people, animals and even plants is that of love. As difficult as it might be to understand, this extraordinary force is slowly beginning to find scientific acceptance.

Dr. Masaru Emoto's work on water and ice crystals provides dramatic visual evidence of the healing power of love. Receiving love is easy, while giving it is more difficult. Natural laws provide an example: If we do not plant seeds, the harvest will not be forthcoming. For the soil to produce that which sustains us, we must first patiently nurture it. In life, we must engage in a similar effort, with equal patience and serenity. As our forefathers said: "From us endeavor, from on high, bountifulness."

We must constantly work to give something back—to our spouses, our children, our friends and to society as a whole. In actual fact, for love to find love we do not have to try to find anything at all. Even when we have no expectations of love in reward, love will always find us. For this is nothing less than the Law of Attraction and the resonance phenomenon.

Each time we sow a seed we must approach the effort with the faith that we will harvest what we sow; this is because the Law of Attraction generates belief. This is not something bound to any particular time or place; this is an absolute concrete belief. The more we give love, the more we shall receive in return and the energy released will increase out potency just as it would from the soil. This is not an empty claim. On the contrary, this law is essential to our happiness in life.

To become a person filled with love, it is not enough just to say "I really love myself." This endeavor requires time and dedication. When that objective is eventually achieved, then we can look at every event in our lives with the right measure of love, and it becomes a natural reflex. As this happens, happiness becomes an inescapable fact of life. Buddha said: "For happiness there is no special way; happiness is the way itself."

As we work on making this a habitual part of our lives there is another pleasurable exercise that we can do. We can keep a daily record of what we do for others, family or non-family. It could be something extra we do for our children in addition to normal parental responsibilities; it could be calmly accepting or even apologizing to our spouses for something that would normally generate an angry response. It could be a small act of charity for those less fortunate. It could be a nice gesture to a friend. It could support for youth development or help for the elderly. The wonderful thing about keeping a record is that we see how it becomes a habitual part of daily life. We begin to seek out worthy action. We begin to think: "What can I do in the way of charity and good works today?" Or "Who can I help today?" When that day arrives and you look back, you will see that you have covered leagues on the way to becoming a human being filled with love.

Remember: in performing these acts of charity for others, we are the beneficiary. Like all efforts to change patterns, this starts with small steps. Before long it becomes an inseparable part of our lives and we are moving forward at great speed.

At the heart of these changes to our behavior lies our close family: our spouses or partners, our parents, our children and our brothers and sisters. Each one has a separate, special place for us, because nearly all of our behavior is shaped by our family environment. As it is essential for us to love and be at peace with ourselves to reap the benefit of love's positive energy, so the bonds of love with our family are equally important in strengthening the network of love and reaching out to humanity. We only have to think of the extreme discomfort caused by a member of our family suffering a physical illness that can even weaken the energy of positive thought within us, so much so that conflict in a family can even bring the positive energy in the universal network of love grinding to a halt!

When a physical disorder of a serious nature is diagnosed, family members rally around the afflicted. But if the disorder is of an emotional or psychological nature, we may find it difficult to maintain the same level of tolerance and concern. We may even find ourselves reproaching our sick relative! If the same concern and tolerance could be extended to mental illness as it is to the physical, it would strengthen the foundations of mutual love within the family. Love is infectious and healing and love attracts love, as we have mentioned many times. To love the one you are with, you have to understand them, which is why we must develop the ability to empathize; we have to put ourselves in their place and we have to be able to look at the world from their perspective. At same time, this creates an environment of tolerance.

Empathy makes it easier to forgive the faults of others. Love and forgiveness are almost interchangeable. Forgiveness is the preparation for love and love the preparation for forgiveness. Just as empathy allows us to understand and forgive others, it also gives us the opportunity to examine our own part in any given argument.

It is a virtue to be able to recognize our own faults. However, after this recognition it is essential that we forgive ourselves, thus removing any barriers to loving ourselves. It will be a continual source of inspiration to loving ourselves if we encounter the universe, including family, friends, strangers—humanity—with our faces glowing and our hearts full of infinite love. There is only one to extricate ourselves from non-love and the secret is in front of our eyes; only "love" can open our hearts.

Those who have implemented this simple axiom "Love yourself and so love others" have been amazed by the results. But there is another aspect to being filled with love and that is the ability to apologize. To be able to breathe deep and apologize after a misunderstanding when angry, hurtful words were uttered is the height of spiritual maturity. How can anyone bear a grudge when they receive a sincere apology? Naturally, done habitually and insincerely, it will lose all meaning.

There is another important insight I want to share with you: the idea that "love constitutes love of the Creator." Most people subscribe to some sort of religious belief; these beliefs ensure that we are closely linked to our Creator. In Sufism there is a saying: "Just as the moth is drawn to the flame and devoured so must we become one with the Creator."

There is a common thread in all religions:
The Creator is all powerful.
The Creator is all mighty.
The Creator is all time and all places.
This endless divine power created us and the universe.

I would like to share a verse sent to me by a friend. It is called "A Life Hoarded Away Like a Golden Coin." The poet's name is unknown but it explains in a different way the significance of love.

When I was in my 20's I set my alarm for 30.
When I was 30 I moved it forward to 40 and then to 50.
How wrongly I have wound up and set my life,
In the morning there is no sleep in my eyes.
I have gained much time to talk,
But now there is nobody left to share these words.
My life has been like a hoarded gold coin,
When the time came to take it from its safe,
I found that it was no longer legal tender…
For all my friends who are still in circulation,
I have but a few words to share,
Give up this stupid rat race,
That's not a shroud in your pocket,
What does wealth, success and power mean,
When you should be really knowing the worth
of the one who loves you?

When the poet wrote 'the one who loves you" we can
assume that he was referring to both friends and to the
Creator. Though hard to visualize, we can perceive the Creator
in the rules and laws of the universal system. This can be at the
individual level of personal morality; we soon know in our
conscience if we have broken the universal laws. This divine
code has existed since ancient times, passed down in different
forms from generation to generation.

"Reap what you sow."
"Do good and you will find good."
"Give and you shall receive."
We could also add: "Loving yourself is loving the Creator."

From this we can see how closely we are bound to our
Creator, which is why we are always so concerned about the
withdrawal of that divine love. If, in our supplications we

combine our love for the Creator with love for ourselves, this love will be embraced by all. Whatever religion we claim, at some point we all feel the need to reach out in our supplications to the Creator and try to live our lives in a seemly manner. Some people might describe this as a fear reflex and anxiety about divine retribution, while others maintain that it is a question of will and conscience. But in the final analysis, it comes down to the belief in "like attracting like," but not one based on short-term benefits. There is a high probability that success will be slow in coming, but with patience and perseverance and by repeating these exercises there is little doubt that you will reach your objective.

One of the principles of loving oneself and becoming a person filled with love is honesty, but it is part of human nature to exploit the expediency of white lies. There are some reasonable explanations; to avoid hurting someone or escalating a crisis. Most of us are not overly troubled by a lie that does not harm anyone. In different research conducted in the United States, almost half of those surveyed report that they do not have a problem with lies. It is likely that similar research in the rest of the world would show similar results. In ancient Greece, for instance, there were schools that instructed students in lying effectively. A similar value system existed in ancient China; any lie told to prevent someone being hurt was considered an act of charity. It even had a name: "innocent lying."

If we accept this evaluation, lying is almost considered a virtue. However, whichever value system we are using, there is no doubt about the true identity of telling lies. Whether one classifies lies as white, gray or black, they are still lies and not the same as honesty. Only in the most extraordinarily sensitive situations should we ever resort to telling white lies with the proviso that it never became a repeated habit. It goes without saying that a white lie can never be perjurious or a criminal offence.

It is not out of fear of divine retribution but out of a sense of divine love that we know that there is a price to pay for every dishonest action. This is because all these events, one way or another, are recorded onto our karma. If these white lies do not disturb the whole identity of our subconscious there will probably be no reduction in our capacity to love ourselves. The real test of our personal integrity is if we can stare into our eyes in the mirror and still consider ourselves honest. Our lips might be able to lie, but the eyes find this impossible.

Another route to becoming filled with love is to increase our loyalty to family and friends. We must first be a "good" person, though. First, ask yourself: "Am I loyal to myself?" Loyalty never means that you expect something in return; that would indicate that you are putting your own self-interest first. Self-interest is like a virus gnawing away at humanity's goodwill. But is there really any chance for anyone to love themselves if they spend their entire existence in the grip of rampant self-interest? If they remain focused only on what will benefit them, they will always be takers and never taste the deep contentment that giving brings.

It is natural that givers find it easier to obtain love and to love themselves. For this reason takers have difficulty making eye contact with their reflection in the mirror, because they know that they will be looking straight into their souls and what is revealed there will be disturbing. It is not just the ability to love themselves that plagues those obsessed with their own self-interest; they have no chance of ever understanding the true meaning of love in any form either.

Some young people are given advice that the only way to survive in this world is to take care of their own self-interest; but in the long run, even the most self-interested, if clever enough, realize they need to take care of other people's interests too. As humanity, with every stumbling step, becomes that bit more refined, that bit more mature, we begin to realize that, in the final analysis, the greatest blessing of all is love. So, as the realization comes that the long term protection of self-interest requires the protection of other people's interests, we will begin to perceive the necessity of loving ourselves and of being a giver and of being filled with love.

As we love we will be loved and we will be able to love our-selves even more, for love attracts love, thus bringing love for ourselves and the ability to love others. We have journeyed from thought to loving ourselves and from there to love itself. We have surveyed and memorized the paths that must be taken on this journey with the purpose of, by loving ourselves, to turn our thoughts into reality. How successful will we be? And if we do all these things will we be able to make are prayers come true? We can only wait and see.

# X

❧

# The Secret's Secret:
# Loving Yourself

If we were to observe humanity from creation to the present we would see that humans have a seemingly endless demand for attention. If our demands are not met, we begin to store away in our subconscious all of our rejections, our failures, and all of the resulting negative emotions. Within time our karma vault starts to overflow with the buildup of negativity. Negative rants become a self-fulfilling prophecy. Discontent returns back to us.

Our demands are invariably directed at the outer world, which is why we pay scant attention to our inner world. We need to understand what we really want from the outer world, what it expects from us, and how we perceive it. We should take great care with enchanting, seductive thoughts and desires lest they enslave us.

Of course, we have come to realize in this age of quantum awareness that what we might perceive as real is not always so, and that while observing what is real we ourselves can undergo a change. In the quantum understanding, the universe came into being as an entirety. We are inseparable parts of the whole. With the frequencies of our thought energy field we are able to connect using the particles of the whole. The defining point is whether our thoughts are negative or positive.

Professor Alan Wolf put it succinctly when he said that with an understanding of the rules and principles of quantum philosophy, we suddenly realize that we are not cornered by any situation. With this understanding we can shape our own reality. In the quantum understanding, the universe came into being as an entirety. We are inseparable parts of the whole. With the frequencies of our thought energy field we are able to connect using the particles of the whole. The defining point is whether our thoughts are negative or positive.

We can turn what we perceive as negative into a positive. Changing what "is" is futile; we must change our perceptions and thus it will be that our own reality is affected and we have affected change. In this way we create a field where we can achieve results for our desires in such a way that we can clear the negativity from our karma. The ultimate objective is to transform our karma into a repository for the positive energy of our thoughts.

Those who are full with positive thought energy are the people with the highest level frequencies of the thought electromagnetic field. Our energy frequencies are controlled by our thoughts and emotions, providing us with limitless energy. If we use this energy wisely there is no obstacle that cannot be overcome. Wherever we focus our vibrations is where our released energy will flow. This is the primary principle of the Law of Attraction that "like attracts like."

Great volumes of material have been written on these subjects. There have been many methods proposed, claims made and arguments put forth to support them. There are numerous examples of the vital importance of positive affirmation to be found. Advice has been offered about the attention we must take with our internal dialogue. However, in all of this information it is rare to find sufficient detail on the initial preparation for the direction of affirmation. Many of these writers seem to imply that if we could only initiate all our wishes and personal development with affirmation, there might be not a single unhappy soul left on earth, but we must remember that if we were to repeat one hundred times each day, "I want to live in the lap of luxury because it is my right to be rich and happy," is there a chance that we would actually become wealthy and contented? Of course not.

As is true of all objectives, when we wish to initiate something we have to take into consideration both the "tricks of the trade" and discover new ways. We can generalize about what it means to be human, but each of us is unique and each of us has our own emotional, psychological and spiritual components. We all carry a unique biological vibration. Each of us needs to work on our own thought matrix in order to see any results.

Despite the shortcomings of many of these self-help sources, many of these provide information that is very useful. For a start, many of them emphasize the importance of love. They use economic language to remind us that: 'thinking positively is loving yourself; love yourself and create miracles in your life." Yes, and we can make our life a miracle if we just love ourselves. This is the essence of the quantum approach. This is why the "Secret's Secret," which is loving yourself, takes on such significance here. It returns to the same critical concept of how we love ourselves.

Some of these sources also teach us how we can use mantras as affirmation matrices to train and prompt our inner world. The dictionary definition of mantra is "freeing the mind." Mantra comes from Sanskrit and can also mean "a sound vibration that can liberate the mind without misdirecting it." In more detail, as a result of reinforcing the thought matrices, the energy bodies reach a level of frequency harmony that puts the entire organism into a state of resonance. Mantras have the power to liberate the aspirations formed in our mind. In quantum terms this signifies the realization of our aspirations.

This comes about from the energy vibrational frequencies produced by our freed aspirations and supplications, resonating within the cosmic void and, through the resonance phenomenon, creating a new reality; thus, affirmation is achieved by using mantras to reinforce our mind with the many reasons for loving ourselves. When a state of loving oneself is attained, the energy level rises accordingly and the aspirational thoughts begin to resonate with frequencies of the universe so that "like attracts like." Energy has the power to turn aspiration into reality.

This is the essence of quantum understanding. As the radio transmitter transmits radio waves that receivers on the same frequency can pick up and reproduce as sound, so thoughts resonate with other thoughts on the same frequency, attracting them and combining their strengths. The quantum understanding is clear on this, "like attracts like." We have already seen how someone who is unable to move their limbs and, just by harnessing the power of their thought, has become able to operate a computer.

Our aspirational energy and frequencies are but a thought away. Love, too, resonates with this thought energy and is an important factor in strengthening and making our aspirations come true. However, we cannot convince our conscious or subconscious of our intentions by blandly saying "I love myself." Only if we know the real reasons behind this love and believe in them will our dreams and aspirations start to come true, one by one. This journey of self-discovery should begin each morning by placing ourselves in front of the mirror. We need to look deep into the real "me" and ask those key questions and, depending upon the answers, decide on how to proceed.

The eyes never lie and, in actual fact, there is a scientific truth to this phrase too. The branch of alternative medicine called iridology bases its approach on the principle that the eyes are not just the mirror of the soul. but of the body's health as well. In the 1950s Dr. Bernard Jensen pioneered iridology by conducting studies on the iris. His studies led him to produce a blueprint that pinpoints the areas of the iris that corresponds to the different parts and organs of the whole body. Thus, it seems correct to say that the eyes are the mirror of everything.

Do you remember what we mentioned about the differences between looking directly into our eyes and avoiding them? There is no doubt that our eyes—the window of our inner world—also look out onto the outer world. Not just our physical body is revealed in our eyes, but our energy bodies as well. Looking deep into our eyes we are able to make observations about our inner worlds. People can be misled, but never by the eyes—never. The eyes that look into the mirror are our outer appearance; the eyes that stare back at us, our inner. So there we are; eye contact has been made and, while keeping it fixed, let us ask the question "Do I love myself?" There are three other questions that we can also ask.

The first is, if we are a "positive" person filled with love. The second is, if we are "holistically honest" towards our body, our emotions, our mind and our spirit. The third is, if we are "benevolent." If we really wish to discover ourselves we should do these exercises regularly, every morning even, and see how we work on the answers when we address that other "me." If we truly direct these questions to our subconscious our responses will be encouraging. We can make this part of our internal daily exercise routine.

We can also use this as a sort of accounts ledger: Whose lives did we have an effect on? Who did we support unconditionally? To whom did we bring some happiness? The size of our contribution is irrelevant, as long as it contributes to loving ourselves. From time to time, glance back through those accounts and see progress. It is probably unnecessary to mention, but the answers to these questions will vary from person to person. It is also possible, if we have habits we want to change, to add additional questions that will help us to achieve this. We should never forget that we all view the world from a different perspective.

The three pillars of loving ourselves remain the same: positive thinking, holistic honesty and benevolence. Anyone who limits themselves to affirmations like, "My life is my work and my objective is to become extremely rich," or "My life is sports and I want to become famous" will, successful or not, find themselves shackled by thinking "The trappings of success is why I love myself." Self-esteem can be a significant factor for successful people, but it is a fleeting form of "loving yourself," based only on their view of their external world. For a love that will last a lifetime there is much more that is required.

If they were only able to look deep into the eyes reflected back at them and were able to sense what was happening in their inner worlds they would realize how empty all of this is and that they would first have to heighten their level of perception. Perhaps they would hear a voice from the depths: "You may have become one of the richest, one of the most famous, one of the most celebrated, but you are not a positive person; you have no interest in being honest with other people and most important of all, you have never done anything for anyone, or if you have it has only been for your own self-interest." If this were the voice inside you, would you still be able to say "I still really love myself"? It would be impossible.

If I can reiterate one more time: It is not your eyes that look out onto the world that are important, it is the eyes that stare back at you from the mirror. It is for that reason that it might be timely to list briefly some of the principles of loving ourselves.

- Positive thinking makes people believe in the power of thought.
- Positive thinking means balanced thinking, the quest for the balance of right, beauty and good.
- Positive thinking gives self-confidence.
- Positive thinking's golden key is equilibrium.
- Positive thinking requires patience and perseverance.
- Positive thinking accepts that everything is in a state of flux, that every success and every sorrow is only temporary.
- Positive thinking accepts that "everything will ascend and finish."

- Positive thinking fills people full of energy, enthusiasm, and excitement.
- Positive thinking focuses thought on the "full" half of the glass.
- Positive thinking makes people become accustomed to thinking what they can give rather than what they can take.
- Positive thinking leads people to believe "you reap what you sow."
- Positive thinking makes people look for the fault first in themselves.
- Positive thinking makes people forgiving and does not foster feelings of revenge.
- Positive thinking removes any sense of remorse about the past or anxiety for the future, but instead, makes people live the moment to the full.
- Positive thinking's most basic precept is to have faith, the compass of the human condition and the palpable and unshakeable bond and trust with the Creator.
- Positive thinking makes people love themselves.

As for the virtues of honesty: we need to examine first how we can be honest in all our bodies: *the physical, the etheric, the emotional, the mental and the meta-physical.* Only when we accomplish this can we possess honesty in its totality. We use a different sense of holistic honesty for each of these bodies. This totality is necessary because the five bodies possess a complex bio-energy field in which they function together. Thus any cause or even any thought energy will influence all the bodies as a totality.

To maintain the honesty of our *physical body* we ask ourselves these questions. We know what we should be doing but are we really doing it? The answers we give determine our level of honesty. When we can answer all of these questions in the affirmative we can be assured that we do have an honest relationship with our physical body.

- Do I follow a good diet?
- Do I provide myself sufficient time for physical exercise?
- Do I avoid tobacco and alcohol?
- Do I have a doctor's check-up at least once a year?
- Do I have regular blood pressure and blood tests and do I monitor the results?

Honesty in our *etheric body* is related to the way we think. If our thoughts are positive it means we are probably able to overcome whatever life throws at us in the way of stress. If we are unable to do this, stress has an extremely detrimental effect on the etheric body. The etheric body, more than the other subtle bodies, functions like a stress station. Stress that affects any one of the bodies affects the others. The most efficacious way of overcoming stress is positive thought. If we are unable to overcome stress and make no effort to do so, we do not have an honest relationship with our etheric body. Anyone heavily burdened with stress will find it hard to love themselves.

Our *emotional body* is the seat in which "love" is found. The virtue of love is in loving ourselves and this disposition starts with approaching everything with a sense of love. The road to love is a long journey because our emotional body is like a windmill turned by the winds of love and this requires effort, patience and perseverance. As our approach to this love slowly becomes part of our disposition, it also makes us more "tolerant." Our usual position, "I am right," changes to "There is no reason for hurt; first let me search within myself." We learn empathy, putting ourselves in the other person's shoes and beginning to understand their point of view, all of which make resolution, understanding and forgiving so much easier. Achieving honesty in our relationship with our emotional body requires us to be full of love and for us accept that even if we really have been wronged, we are mature enough to ignore it.

The golden key to honesty in our *mental body* is "equilibrium." The mental body acts as a balance or bridge between the emotional and the spiritual bodies. The mind has the function of seeking out how equilibrium can be sustained. Establishing a balance between our inner and outer worlds is, in one sense, the duty of our minds. However much our emotional bodies need love, the most important nutrition for our mental bodies is equilibrium. The concept of equilibrium is a careful indication of the sensitive relationship between the outer world and the psychological one. To achieve a satisfactory level of equilibrium depends on how much time we can dedicate to developing these two poles of the balance. It is impossible to talk of mental honesty when referring to the unbalanced, because if there is a conscious effort made to avoid seeking out equilibrium then a position emerges that is light years away from honesty.

When it comes to the spiritual body, the emphasis is on karma; the focus of honesty in all of the bodies is focused on this concept acting as a form of accounting system. To achieve an honest spiritual body it is essential that all negativity is eliminated from our karma. Negative karma develops as a result of negative acts and positive as a result of positive ones. Negative memories of past events and mistakes are accounted in our conscience and manifest themselves as a buildup of negative karma. It does not matter how healthy our other bodies might be; if our spiritual body is filled with negative karma, it is as impossible to discuss the health of our total well-being as it is of holistic honesty. Because all the karmic information is also found in all the other bodies, we can also speak of "total conscious." We must confront the unresolved negative events of our karma and with our own unstinting efforts bring them out into the light of day.

Both psychiatry and medical hypnosis have been successful in finding cosmic blockages and resolving karmic disorders. If we do not wish to resort to these methods then we must start to forgive ourselves and others. We can overcome negativity of the past with love, but first we must look for and identify our faults and decide what we can learn from our mistakes.

We must remember that life is not fair and that other people are victims too. Just as our health never forgives neglect, so life never forgives laziness, imbalance, negativity, disaffection and faithlessness. In place of negativity we should learn to value the positive values we are now discovering in our lives. Our soul needs to rejoice in thanksgiving and we must make a point of rewarding ourselves with these emotions. Very briefly, spiritual honesty means cleansing of the karma.

The basic honesty components of the five bodies

• The physical body / Good diet
• The etheric body / The ability and striving to overcome stress
• The emotional body / Love
• The mental body / Balance
• The spiritual body / Karma cleansing

These components form a totality from their strong opposing characteristics that can be identified as total or holistic honesty. These five elements are interconnected and in harmony, thus constituting the paradigm of our holistic honesty. If we neglect even one of these principles, the path to loving ourselves will be rocky.

We have been looking at the reflection of our eyes in the mirror and attempting to find answers to two of the three questions that we asked ourselves at the beginning. The first question was if we were someone filled with love and the second concerned our holistic honesty. And now to examine the third question and see what can be done there. Let us imagine that our eyes reflected in the mirror bestow their approval. "Yes, we are a positive person; we have also been successful with our holistic honesty and the path we are on is a good one." Will this still be enough to say that we loved ourselves in the complete meaning of that phrase? Perhaps most would say

"Yes, why not," and not be far from the truth. But we should return to the difference between "I love myself" and "I really love myself." It is similar to liking apple pie and ice-cream but actually preferring the ice-cream the most.

If we want to move up to the "I really love myself" category we have to be an example of total benevolence and charity. Humankind is tightly bound to its own self-interest. Yes, we can think positively, be empathetic, be aware of the importance of love and equilibrium, but, apart from the odd occasion of charity, our own self-interests will be blinking like a beacon in the corner of our minds. In order to bring a sustained equilibrium to this situation we have to start thinking more about others than we do about ourselves. Similar to the issue of maintaining a sustained love, we have to share our affection between ourselves and others, but now we see that there is a more elevated level and that, without reconciling our interests, we can reach a higher love. And this is where we learn to give without expecting anything in return.

We can learn to love ourselves strongly and, by using the "Secret's Secret," be able to harness enough high energy from the cosmic resonance of our thoughts and, as a consequence of this, we can unconditionally interconnect with people we know and those we do not, with those we care for and those we do not and thus become generous, charitable and benevolent human beings and cover even greater distances on this voyage of discovery. We have to wholeheartedly believe in the veracity of unconditional giving. We should never have the 'secret" of "like attracts like" far from our minds and we have to totally believe that whatever act of charity or benevolence we do will, one way or another, return to us bountifully many times over. To summarize: the illuminated path to a life full of contentment comes with complete faith in the "Law of Attraction," and that our aspirations are made real with "resonance" and with "loving ourselves."

Thus, this glorious and mysterious journey is but a passage through "the Secret's Secret Secret."

# Conclusion

Ever since I was a child I have had a deep fascination, I must confess sometimes bordering on obsession, in discovering the true nature of the Creator. It is an interest that has remained unabated, almost like the spirit of discovery that drove the ancient Chinese explorers to discover the world. Even if we consider that, from a scientific point of view, it is a hopeless quest; it has not stopped people like myself from seeking this out for thousands of years. Against all the odds and with great application, prophets, theologians and philosophers have brought us closer with interpretations and explanations of the rules and laws of the divine system. This attempt at clarity is something that continues even in our own time. One of the best examples of this is the CERN project and the attempt to isolate and understand what has been dubbed the "God Particle." The researchers are attempting to recreate the moment of creation and in doing so open up a debate and even present "evidence" to the world at large.

We are still far from understanding the Creator's nature, but we are getting a better understanding of the rules and laws and the divine system itself. With the development of quantum physics and the philosophical interpretations that followed, our perception of the world and even the universe, has irreversibly changed.

But while these perceptions have changed, for many of us without sufficient grounding in the subject, the extreme complexity of these new perspectives have made it very difficult for us to visualize or fully comprehend the implications involved. The concept of reality has changed from the "definitive" to being one of flexible relativism. While we once considered there to be one sole reality, we now understand that everyone experiences their own separate realities. This is a concept so difficult to perceive and comprehend that many of us have been left confused. When once we thought of the whole as being made up of its components and, as result fell short of fully comprehending it, we are now beginning to understand that existence is far larger and all encompassing than we had ever before imagined. However, despite the complexity, we are now far better equipped to begin to truly understand ourselves and by association, the universe.

It is for this reason that the Law of Attraction first caught my attention and in this book I have tried to explain the importance of approaching the health of our bodies, the physical health, the emotional health, the mental health and the spiritual health, from the holistic, complete and whole, perspective; at the same time I have discussed natural laws, in particular the Law of Attraction, and how we can harness its power and the strength that lies within us by using resonation. The related research and contents of this book will help us discover what an extraordinary creation we all are and bring us to an entirely new awareness.

The power and abilities within us have always been there, but how do we get them to resonate? How can we access these extraordinary powers and abilities within us? How can we use them to realize our aspirations for the good and beautiful? How can we become more healthy and positive and holistically aware? What approaches should we use to make our dreams, desires and supplications come true? What exactly is the power hidden within us that is manifested by the resonance of the Law of Attraction? How can we increase the level of energy with love?

I have attempted to answer all of these questions by drawing on original research and then explaining it in a way that is accessible to all. This was the reason I took such pains to give the scientific explanation for the Law of Attraction for I am aware that there are still many people who equate this concept with gravitational attraction. However, when we approach it from a quantum physics perspective, we see the difference between the two effects. Despite this, and even with such frequent references to the Law of Attraction, I have yet to come across any another attempt to give it a scientific explanation.

In the course of my research I discovered that, though known since esoteric times, the Law of Attraction and the resonance phenomenon were defined for the first time by Samuel Hahnemann in the 18th century. Hahnemann described it as "like attracts like and cures" and this was the principle for the homeopathic remedies that he pioneered. Despite this, Hahnemann never made the connection that homeopathy was a resonance phenomenon. In this book I have attempted to show how the Law of Attraction is very much a resonance phenomenon and, although perhaps pioneering in its premise, I have researched and backed it up with the relevant empirical evidence.

Although considered a secret for a long time, demonstrating that the Law of Attraction was a resonance phenomenon was aided by using the results of research conducted by a number of scientists into the resonance phenomenon as my examples. To put it briefly, through the pages of this book the Law of Attraction, "like attracts like" has been proven to be a resonance phenomenon purely by the weight of existing scientific evidence.

Carrying on from this point, we touched on the importance of affirmation. We looked at the recent work of Dr. Herbert Benson of the Harvard Medical Faculty, who has shown that the immune system can be strengthened, pulse regulated and depression restrained all by the power of prayer. Dr. Benson stressed that religious denomination was immaterial but that prayer was the most effective and cost-free treatment for arresting the development of illness and aiding recovery. Dr. Benson concluded by saying that just expressing our thanks for our contentment and happiness to our family and wider society could have just the same effect as prayer. In a book produced by the Mayo Clinic's specialists called *On Healty Aging*, the authors draw the same conclusion about the benefits of affirmation and prayer.

It was at that point that we were careful to emphasize that "resonance" could not be achieved by affirmation alone. We stressed that the secret to resonance was to "love ourselves" and spoke of the effect that resonance energy had on our bodies. We attempted to elaborate on how loving ourselves could dramatically increase our energy levels and accelerate our power to resonate. By a natural progression we touched on the ways to reach universal love and, when resonance energy has been tapped into, the extraordinary power of "love."

To emphasize the importance of the power of love, we discussed the three cornerstones of the universe touching on "information" first. From there we progressed to the details of vibrational medicine and how it is a form of bio-informational medicine and from there to the subtle bodies, approaching each one of them in turn. After demonstrating that resonance was a phenomenon of bio-informational medicine we showed that only when the correct information has been collected can the appropriate scientific approach and synthesis be applied.

We discussed the fact that for affirmation to be truly effective, it is vitally important for the individual to be charged with high energy and the necessary methodology and the power of love to achieve this.

We then underlined the importance and preconditions of the health of our different bodies and when sufficient energy levels have been reached, how we are to utilize resonance. The scientific aspects of resonance were also touched on.

We next concluded that only by loving ourselves could all our supplications, wishes, desires and aspirations be realized and how unconditional love is an essential part of this and then, and only then, could resonance be achieved.

It is for this reason that the Secret's Secret is nothing more than "resonance" itself, and the secret of being able to resonate is nothing less than the unconditional "love of oneself."

Our objective has been to make everyone aware of the extraordinary power we hold within ourselves, and to mobilize them into becoming the bridge between conventional and complementary medicine, and to contribute to the ideal of everyone having access to the possibility of a healthy, contented and high quality way of living. If we can get anywhere near this objective, who knows what happiness lies in wait for us.

By touching on the resonance of divine justice, mechanical resonance, biological and morphic resonance and, by association, the secret of the Law of Attraction, we have conceptualized this popular phenomenon and, for the first time, have used analytical data to provide it with a scientific footing. I would like to conclude with the wish that you may always think of roses, and that your life may become a rose garden.

# Glossary

**A**

Affirmation: Positive expressions.

Allopathic: Conventional pharmaceuticals as opposed to homeopathic remedies.

Anti-inflammatory: Drugs that reduce temperature in situations such as fever.

Anti-matter: A term coined after experiments in quantum physics labs revealed the existence of opposites to the atomic particles—anti-electrons, anti-neutrons and anti-protons—and that these anti-particles combine to form antimatter.

Antipyretic: Drug for reducing temperature such as in fever.

Astral projection: Episodes of out-of-body experiences considered to involve an astral counterpart that separates from the body and travels to various astral planes.

Atheism: A belief that no God or gods exist or have yet been proved to exist.

Aura: A term used in metaphysics that describes the radiation from living entities of electromagnetic waves that sometimes form layers of light or color around the body.

# B

Bach flower therapy: A complementary form of medicine based on the belief that the majority of illnesses do not originate from physical causes but from emotional or mental ones such as phobias, anxiety, irrationality and exhaustion. These are treated with preparations made from various flowers and plants.

Bio-feedback: A form of complementary medicine whereby the patient's bodily functions readings are used in a transfer of data.

Biological frequencies. The frequency values pertaining to the body or the bodily functions.

Biological resonance therapy: A method of correcting the patient's bodily frequencies by the retransmission of stimuli back to the body so that it has the capacity to heal itself.

# C

Collagen: The body's most commonly found building block protein.

# D

Deism: A theological view that although the universe was created by a Divine Being, there has never been, or will be, further divine intervention.

Detoxification: Removing toxins from the body.

# E

Einstein paradigm: Meaning the vibrational medicine paradigm, whereby the human organism is made up of a series of interconnected networks starting at particle level through to cellular levels and beyond.

Elastin: A basic component of connective tissue and one of the scleroproteins.

Electromagnetic: A fundamental force combining the properties of electricity and magnetism. An electromagnetic field is charged with static electricity thus creating a force. It is created peripherally by electrical current passing through a conductor (like electrical cable).

Epigenesis: The stage in which, following the uniting of sperm and ovum, the embryo begins to be formed.

Etheric body: The name given in esotericism and neo-theosophy to the first and lowest level of the aura.

Esotericism: Implies the imparting of secrets. It is not a religion or belief system.

**F**

FMRI: Functional Magnetic Resonance Imaging.

**G**

Gestalt theory. A psychological approach whereby the whole being, biological as well as psychological, is taken into consideration.

Glucosamine: An amino derivative of glucose manufactured by the body but also found in small amount in some food stuffs; plays an important role in protecting connective tissue.

**H**

Hemodialysis: A technique using semi-porous membrane (dialysis) to mechanically remove waste from the blood in the case of renal failure.

Hertz: The unit of frequency.

Holistic: The whole.

Holistic medicine: A branch of complementary medicine that evaluates the physical, mental and spiritual body as a whole.

Holography: A technique for recording, and then reconstructing, the amplitude and phase distributions of a coherent wave disturbance; used to produce three-dimensional images or holograms.

Hologram: A 3D image made from the information garnered from electromagnetic laser amplitude and phase illumination.

Hologenesis: The hypothesis that humankind appeared all over the earth at the same time.

Homeopathy: A system of treating diseases with small amounts of substances that, in larger amounts, would produce the observed symptoms.


I

Infoseuticals: Is a branch of complementary medicine that differs from homeopathic remedies in that the preparations are injected with amplitude and phase vibrational information by various methods and equipment.

Iridology: A branch of complementary medicine whereby diagnosis is done by examining the iris of the eye.


K

Karma: Originating in Eastern religions, a belief that your actions determine you fate.

Kinesiology: A diagnostic method of examining bodily movements to determine causes and possible treatment options.

Kirlian photography: The name given to an electrographic photographic technique whereby high voltage, high frequency but low amperage electricity is used by equipment to record biological radiation from living organisms photographically.

**L**

Levitation: The rising or causing to rise in the air, which is usually attributed to supernatural intervention.

Lymphatic system: a network of lymphatic vessels and lymph nodes that transport fluid, fats, proteins, and lymphocytes to the bloodstream as lymph, and remove microorganisms and other debris from tissues.

**M**

Matrix: A number of meanings including template and network, but in particular the connective tissue consisting of elastin, collagen and glucosamine that connects the circulatory, nervous and lymphatic systems as well as providing nutrients to the cells of organs.

Morphic field: Separate from concepts of energy and matter, it is a subtle field that has an organizational role in all systems.

Morphic resonance: The hypothesis that all organisms' past form and behavior have direct effect on the organisms that follow.

Morphogenesis: The laws that govern the development and form of tissue and organs in living organisms.

Morphology: The study of the form and structure of animals and plants.

Mitochondrion: A spherical or ovoid organelle found in the

cytoplasm of eukaryotic cells, contains genetic material separate from that of the host; it is responsible for the conversion of food to usable energy in the form of ATP.


# N

Nadis: Energy channels (Eastern esotericism)

Nosodes: A complementary medical method using preparations similar to those of homeopathy although instead of plant or mineral basis, material from infected organs, urine, blood tissue etc., is used.


# O

Orthodox medicine: Conventional or Western medical practice as taught in major teaching hospitals. The standard practice in most hospitals worldwide.

# P

Pantheism: A philosophical view that the whole universe and everything in it is the one Divine Being.

Paradigm: A series of values.

Paramagnetic: Objects when placed in a magnetic field temporarily take on magnetic characteristics.

Parapsychology: The study of that which cannot yet be explained; psychic or occult phenomena, such as telepathy etc.

Pathogen: An organism causing disease.

Petechia: a small spot, especially on an organ, caused by bleeding underneath the membrane or skin.

pH value: The acidity/alkali level of a solution based on H+ ion concentration.

Pharmacologist: Someone who studies the preparation, application and effects of pharmaceuticals.

Pharmaceuticals: Conventional medication.

Philo-physicist: One who combines the science of existence with philosophical elements and tries to find the reasoning between intelligence and physical events.

Photon: The quantum of light and other electromagnetic energy, regarded as a discrete particle having zero rest mass, no electric charge, and an indefinitely long lifetime. It is a gauge boson.

Polarity: The separation, alignment or orientation of something into two opposed poles.

Potential field: A field that is devoid of power in its current form, but possesses a latent form that gives it the capacity to be developed and exploited.

Prebiotics: In simple terms, the foods needed to be eaten to provide the best environment for probiotics to live and function.

Probiotics: Friendly bacteria found in the intestines that maintain the balance of flora and hostile bacteria. These are essential for control of candiasis and a healthy intestinal tract.


# Q

Quantum: Derived from the Latin for "how much," it is the smallest possible, and therefore indivisible, unit of a given quantity or quantifiable phenomenon


# R

Radiation: The transmission of heat or energy from a specific source. It is transmitted by particle oscillation or vibration.

Resonance repatterning: "Reorganizing anew by resonance." Eliminating negative beliefs, behavior, thoughts and emotions from our lives.

Resonance: Occurs when there is an external frequency, the same as the natural frequency, that stimulates a strong harmonic response. If the frequency is the same the effect is constructive or stimulating. If the frequency is opposing there is a destructive and damaging effect.

## S

Symptomatic drugs: Drugs designed and prescribed for a specific symptom.

SIT: System Information Therapy, cf., Biological Resonance Therapy.

Synbiotics: Preparations that combine the properties of both pre and probiotics.

Synergy: The more effective, constructive and powerful working together of units, as compared to that of a sole unit, as one rather than individually.

Subtle bodies: Found in esoteric, occult and mystic teaching to describe the hierarchy and levels of the psycho-spiritual body's energy fields.

Sub-atomic particles: The smaller components of the atom (electron, proton, neutron, bosons etc.).

## T

Theism: A religious philosophy based on an interventionist creator.

Telekinesis: The movement of a body caused by thought or willpower without application of a physical force.

Telepathy: The communication between people of thoughts, feelings, desires etc. involving mechanisms that cannot be understood in terms of known scientific laws.

Theory of relativity: A theory that contends that both time and speed are relative and that time and space are only relative properties of a material universe.

Theosophy: A field of thought originating from Eastern mysticism, that was combined with Western occult traditions in an attempt to understand the relationship between the divine and the universe. Theosophy was founded on three principles:

1. To form a nucleus of the Universal Brotherhood of Humanity, without distinction of race, creed, sex, caste, or color.

2. To encourage the study of Comparative Religion, Philosophy, and Science.

3. To investigate the unexplained laws of Nature and the powers latent in man.

# Y

Yin-Yang: According to Chinese philosophy, yin and yang are complementary opposites within a greater whole. Everything has both yin and yang aspects, which constantly interact, never existing in absolute stasis.

# Bibliography

Andrews, T., *Aura*, İstanbul: Mete, 2003.

Batie, H. F., *Healing Body, Mind & Spirit*, St. Paul MN: Llewellyn, 2003.

Batmanghelidj, F., *Water*, New York: Warner, 2003.

Becker, R. O., *The Body Electric*, New York: William Morrow, 1985.

Byrne, R., *Secret*, Oregon: TS Production, 2006.

Candan, E., *Son Üç Peygamber*, İstanbul: Sinir Ötesi, 2002.

Çiller, Ö. U., *Mutlu ve Başarılı Olma Sanatı*, İstanbul: İnkilap, 1990.

Çiller, Ö. U., *Pencere*, İstanbul: Truva, 2005.

D'Anna, S. E., *Tanrılar Okulu*, İstanbul: GOA, 2008.

Davis, M., *Rainbows of Life*, New York: Harper, 1978.

Dawkins, R., *Tanrı Yanılgısı*, İstanbul: Kuzey, 2008.

Emoto, M., *Love Thyself*, Carlsbad, CA: Hay House, 2004.

Fischer, G., *Living Systems Information Therapy* (Introduction to Quantum Medicine), Niebüll, Verlag videel OHG, 2003.

Fraser, P. H., *Decoding the Human Body-Field*, Rochester Vermont: Healing Arts, 2008.

Freitag, E. F., *Bilinmeyenden Yardım*, İstanbul: Omega, 2004.

Gerber, R., *Vibrational Medicine*, New York: Harper, 2000.

Grof, S., *Kozmik Oyun*, İstanbul: Dönüşüm, 2002.

Gün, N., *Çekim Yasası*, İstanbul: Nil Gün, 2007.

Harra, C., *Everyday Karma*, New York: Random, 2002.

Hawkins, D. R., *Power vs Force*, Carlsbad CA: Hay House, 2002.

Hay, L. L., *Tüm Hastalıkların Zihinsel Nedenleri*, İstanbul: Akaşa, 2000.

Jamal, A., *Gündelik Hayatta Mevlânâ ve Sufizm*, İstanbul: Pegasus, 2007.

Mann, M., *Become What You Believe*, Vermont: Society of Pragmatic Mysticism, 1970.

Maurer, H., *The Principle of Existence*, Graz Austria: Norderstedt, 2007.

Merter, M., *Dokuz Yüz Katlı İnsan*, İstanbul: Kaktüs, 2007.

Paulson, G. L., *Kundalini and the Chakras*, St. Paul MN: Llewellyn, 2003.

Sheldrake, R., *A New Science of Life: The Hypothesis of Morphic Resonance*, Rochester Vermont: Park Street, 1995.

228 Talbot, M., *Holografik Evren*, İstanbul: Ruh ve Madde, 2004.

Taylor, J. R., *The Wonder of Probiotics*, New York: Lynn Sonberg, 2007.

Wolf, F. A., *Düşünceyi Gerçeğe Dönüştürmek*, İstanbul: MIA, 2007.

Wordsworth, C., *Quantum Change Made Easy*, Arizona: Resonance, 2007.

# Özer Uçuran Çiller's
# Published Books to Date:

- *Mutlu ve Başarılı Olma Sanatı* (The Art of Happiness and Success), 1990.

- *Yeniçağda Düşünce Gücü ve Holistik Sağlığa Açılan Pencere* (The Power of Thought in the New Age and the Window Opening onto Holistic Health), 2005.

- *Sırrın Sırrı* (The Secret of the Secret), 2009.

- *Yazgı: Değişken Kader* (Predestination: Variable fate), 2010.

- *İnfotheism: Tanrı'nın Enformasyonu* (Infotheism: God's Information), 2011.

- *Mutlu, Huzurlu, Başarılı Olabilme Sanatı* (The Art of Being Happy, Contented, and Successful), 2011.